Trends in Linguistics

Studies and Monographs

edited by

W. Winter

University of Kiel, Germany

2

TAGMEMICS
Volume 2
THEORETICAL DISCUSSION

edited by

Ruth M. Brend
and
Kenneth L. Pike

1976

MOUTON

THE HAGUE - PARIS

ISBN 90 279 3425 8

Printed in the Netherlands

PREFACE

To the Two Companion Volumes on Tagmemics

In these two volumes we have endeavored to cover a number of the current theoretical concerns of tagmemicists by inviting persons who have actively contributed to various parts of the theory to write on them. Each author of the included chapters has published within the immediate past, one or more works on the areas he or she discusses and, in varying degrees, the chapter indicates the author's current thinking and gives some indication of his or her current and future research. The authors are not completely unified in their perspectives but, rather, show some of the varying views held by persons working with the theory.

These volumes, however, do not cover all of the areas currently being investigated by tagmemicists: for example, little mention is made of the application of mathematical group theory.[1] Also, although 'matrix' or 'field' theory is mentioned by several of the authors, its application to sub-morphemic constants is not covered at all.[2] In addition, the application of tagmemic theory to various peripheral areas such as music, psychotherapy, pedagogy, etc., is barely mentioned. Summaries of these and other areas of tagmemic research, not covered in these volumes may be found in publications of Viola Waterhouse,[3] Kenneth L. Pike,[4] and Ruth M. Brend.[5] And of course, details of work in progress by virtually all of the authors[6] have not been included.

Rather than a broad summary of all tagmemic research, therefore, we present here some of the results of tagmemic scholarship and some current directions of research, plus a considerable amount of theoretical discussion.

In the first volume, Robert Longacre (who himself has thus far been the inspirer and publisher of the majority of the tagmemic studies of discourse) summarizes the historical development of discourse analysis from the inception of the theory to the present, and he poses provocative questions regarding where the attention of scholars must now be placed. Eunice Pike gives a number of distinctive concepts of tagmemic phonology (to which she herself has contributed) and summarizes the research in this area. Mary Ruth Wise, in her chapter on language and behavior demonstrates that relationships between verbal and non-verbal behavior have been considered central to tagmemics and she summarizes the already extensive research on this topic, citing a wide range of publications.

In the second volume, Peter Fries has organized his chapter around distinctions between surface versus underlying structure being made by a number of tagmemicists. He cites, in particular, publications related to this theme which describe syntactic levels below that of discourse. Austin Hale, whose training and earlier work has been chiefly as a transformational grammarian, discusses the place of rules and derivation within tagmemic theory and mentions some relationships between that theory and transformational grammar. Finally, Kenneth Pike presents some crucial tagmemic concepts, with a historical comment as to their inception and development, and then suggests a set of postulates to indicate some logical connections between those concepts.

The first volume, therefore, is largely a summary of language descriptions utilizing the theory, with a lesser amount of theoretical discussion than is found in the second volume. Together, however, these volumes present, we believe, a good summary of the state of some of the major areas of tagmemic research today.

Ruth M. Brend
Kenneth L. Pike
February, 1976

FOOTNOTES

1 See, for example, Kenneth L. Pike and Ivan Lowe, 'Pronominal Reference in English Conversation and Discourse: a Group Theoretical Treatment, ' *Folia Linguistica* 3, 68-106 (1969), and Ivan Lowe, 'An Algebraic Theory of English Pronominal Reference (Part I),' *Semiotica* 1, 397-421 (1969).
2 One of several publications in this area is by Kenneth Pike and Barbara Erickson Hollenbach, 'Conflated Field Structures in Potawatomi and in Arabic,' *International Journal of American Linguistics*, 30.201-212 (1964).
3 *The History and Development of Tagmemics*, The Hague: Mouton, (1974).
4 'A Guide to Publications Related to Tagmemic Theory,' *Current Trends in Linguistics* (ed. T. A. Sebeok) 3 The Hague: Mouton, pp. 365-94 (1966).
5 'Tagmemic theory: an Annotated Bibliography, (plus Appendix I),' *Journal of English Linguistics*, 4.7-45; 6.1-16. (1970, 1972).
6 For example a major pedagogical volume in preparation by Kenneth and Evelyn Pike to be published by the Summer Institute of Linguistics this year and a volume on discourse in preparation by Robert Longacre.

TABLE OF CONTENTS

viii

ON SURFACE AND UNDERLYING STRUCTURE, WITH SPECIAL REFERENCE TO PHRASE, CLAUSE AND SENTENCE

PETER HOWARD FRIES

Central Michigan University

SECTION I

Language is a part of behavior. It operates within a matrix of non-verbal behavior and interacts with non-verbal behavior in intimate ways. A transcript of what basketball players say to each other on the court during a game would be unintelligible if it did not also describe the physical activities going on at the time. Similarly, it is often inappropriate to give a purely verbal reply to speech. To the request *Can you open the window?* it is quite inappropriate to reply *Yes* without, in fact, opening the window. It is therefore necessary that a framework of analysis be applied to language which is also applicable to the description of non-verbal behavior.

One of the fundamental attributes of behavior is that it has purpose. We do not do things randomly. We act in order to achieve certain ends and goals. We can thus distinguish between the physical act and the goal that act is to achieve; or, in other words, between the form and the function of each act. Most of human behavior is very complex, however, and what can be seen on one level as a single behavior oriented toward achieving a single purpose, can be seen on another level to be a complex of activities each intended to attain a subgoal of the overall purpose of the activity. A person, for example, may wish to enjoy himself in the company of his friends, and therefore engages in a game of bridge. Thus, bridge is an activity that has the function in this case of contributing to someone's enjoyment. On another level of analysis, however, bridge is a complex of activities such as dealing, bidding, laying out the cards of the dummy, and playing the hand. Each of these has a function within the game of bridge.

Language fits into this overall behavioral framework in much the same way as bridge does. In each instance language is used to achieve a behavioral goal: it may be used to bid in a game, or to narrate an event, or to turn someone down, or to tell a wellknown story in an artistically satisfying way. Varied as these functions are, they all involve the communication of meaning of some

2

sort. As a result, we can say that the major function of language is the communication of meaning. However, an utterance is not merely a sequence of small units each having its own meaning, with the meaning of the total unit equal to the sum total of the meanings of the individual units. Like the rest of behavior, language behavior is a hierarchy of behaviors. On an overall view (level), what one says is the form of language, while what one means by what he says is the function of language. But, like bridge, speaking is a major task which has within it subtasks. Each of these subtasks plays some sort of role (function) within a major task of speaking, and each of these subtasks is related to the overall task via a functional relationship. Thus, within the grammar of language, we will find at least two kinds of functional relations; grammatical functions, which are functions of elements of the form of language, and the communication of meanings, which is the function of language as a whole.

So far we have focussed only on the functional aspect of language, but clearly, if a unit is to function, it must have some physical manifestation. In other words, units must have form. Tagmemicists have been fairly literal in their interpretation of this statement, and deal primarilly only with units which have overt form. Occasionally, in certain specified situations, they are forced to treat units which do not have form. They have, for example, traditionally opposed the use of zero morphemes (see Elson and Pickett, 1962:20 and Longacre 1964:106). They will, however, when confronted by a strong morphological pattern occasionally deal with a zero unit. Thus a morphological matrix in which all cells except one are filled may be said to contain a zero formative.

Similarly, tagmemicists have traditionally opposed the use of deleted elements. They thus object to many of the abstract representations suggested by transformational grammarians. (e.g. their analyses involving abstract performative and causative verbs). They will, however, if necessary, treat units which fill more than one function. (Such analyses will account for a few of the less abstract cases of transformational deletion). Thus in the noun phrase *the boy I knew* one can say that the noun which fills the head function of the noun phrase (*boy*) also fills the object function of the relative clause. That is, instead of saying that an element has been deleted from the relative clause, tagmemicists prefer to say that a certain specified element in the environment does double duty.

In tagmemic theory, then, units are correlations of form and meaning. While they must have form, they are not the form.

...our present theory would not allow us to say – when we are on our guard, or consistent – that a linguistic item "is the bearer of a meaning," since there would be no available linguistic units to 'bear' meanings, in view of the fact that there are only form-meaning composites. (Pike 1967:1963)

In addition the correlation between form and meaning is thought to be relatively direct.[1] Pike has told me that in his mind, one of the greatest differences between stratificational grammar and tagmemics lies in the fact that tagmemics assumes a direct relation between form and meaning while stratificational grammar does not. As a result, many features tagmemicists, Pike in particular, consider to be closely related (and hence features which are dealt with at one location within tagmemic grammars), often are dealt with in widely disparate parts of stratificational grammars.

Tagmemics, then, is a model of behavior in which units are basic. Except in very special cases, all units must be directly relatable to some formal expression, and must fill some function. Within language, units have two types of functions; one, meaning, is a part of the total overall function of language. Each unit, or subunit, makes its contribution to the meaning of the overall meaning of the larger unit of which it is a part. The second, grammatical function, is the function a unit has within larger units of language.

Though we have drawn the distinction in the previous paragraph between meaning and grammatical function, it would be false to draw the conclusion that grammatical functions do not contribute to the meaning of a unit. In fact, grammatical functions make a very special contribution to the meanings of the units of which they are parts. A given situation, for example, may be reported in either of the following two ways: a) *Bill came early. That surprised Mary.* or b) *Bill's coming early surprised Mary.* Both a) and b) describe the same situation. That is, they convey the same situational meaning. They differ in the manner in which they convey this information, however. The first method of expressing the message seems to say that there are two events which happen to be related. This is indicated by the fact that the message is conveyed in the form of two independent sentences and the only formal signal relating the two is the anaphoric use of *that* in the second sentence to refer to the first sentence. This method of expression is likely to be used when the speaker believes that both events are equally new information to the listener and that they are of roughly equal importance.

The second method of expressing the message seems to say that there is one event which happens to contain another as a part of it. This is indicated by the grammatical fact that the subject of the main clause is a nominalized clause. This method of expression is likely to be used when the speaker believes that the listener already knows that Bill came early, so that the focus of the total predication is on the effect of this event on Mary. In other words, the grammatical functions used to express a given situational meaning determine the focus or emphasis put on that meaning. They do this partially directly and partially by determining the unit types which are used to express the meanings.

From what has been said it should be obvious that in the discussion of language we must deal at least with grammatical form, grammatical function, and situational meaning. All tagmemicists agree that grammatical form and grammatical function are closely related. There is disagreement on how closely situational meaning is to be associated with the two, however. In the following sections I will begin by discussing the grammatical aspect of language and then the semantic (or lexemic) aspect and finally the relations between the two. In the last section I will show the formalisms which have been developed to describe the various facets of language discussed.

This sequence betrays my underlying sympathy for Longacre's basic approach to the description of language in which the grammatical and lexemic aspects of language are relatively independent. He writes, for example,

It is evident that just as we must have a general taxonomy of deep structure (with the possibility of adapting slightly the general scheme in order to make it specific to a given language), so we must also have a taxonomy of the surface structure of a given language. If we are to map deep structures onto surface structures in a language, so that a particular deep structure r can be said to encode as either g, g', or g" in the surface structure, then r must have its taxonomic placement in the deep structure and g, g', and g" must have their taxonomic placement in the surface structures of that language. (1972:93)

Similarly a few pages before he says

... there is no neccessary correspondence between deep and surface structure... (1972:82)

While I can find no place that Longacre explicitly says so, the passages just quoted necessarily imply that the units and functions of the surface grammar are independent of deep structure units and functions, and vice versa.[2]

The sequence I am taking has the added advantage that it mirrors the history of the development of tagmemics. By the mid 1960's, when tagmemicists became seriously interested in integrating semantic structure into their theory, their approach to the description of surface structure was pretty well developed. By introducing this portion of the history first, I can introduce the technical terms of the theory in their traditional meanings and cite portions of the writings of those times without either changing the original terms used or introducing an undue amount of confusion through using the terms to express several meanings in the same section.

In the later sections of this chapter I will show how the meanings of these terms have been modified in the last few years.

SECTION II

There are five fundamental concepts within the tagmemic approach to grammar: *tagmeme, syntagmeme, system,*[3] *level,* and *hierarchy.* Let me discuss each of these terms in turn.[4]

A tagmeme is an association of a grammatical function with the set of items which may fill that function. As Longacre has said,

Tagmemics makes grammatical functions focal, but associates such functions with sets of items and constructions (1965:65)

The primacy of grammatical function arises because the various functions contribute a type of meaning. Thus the subject of a clause is the topic of the clause. *John saw Bill* is a statement about John, while *Bill was seen by John* is a statement about Bill. Similarly, *the dented fender* is not an exact paraphrase of *the fender dented.* (*The dented fender was the left one. The fender dented was the left one.*) When the participle occurs before the noun, it characterizes the noun in a relatively permanent way. When the participle follows the noun it modifies no such permanence is implied.[5] The difference in the relationship between modifier and head in the two examples above results from the difference in the grammatical functions the two modifiers fill.

Differences in functional relationships are formally demonstrable in that they correlate with differences in form: e.g. different filler classes, permutability, transformation potential, agreement, etc. It is important to note, however, that these formal correlates do not define the function but only correlate with the function. A grammatical function is a relationship between a constituent and the construction of which it is a part. The formal correlates of a grammatical function are not the relationship itself, but a result of such a relationship.

Since a grammatical function is a relationship between a constituent of a construction and the construction itself, to speak of a grammatical function implies the existence of some unit which contains the function. Such units are called syntagmemes. But the units of language are contrastive units, thus syntagmemes are contrastive construction types. Contrast here does not refer to contrast in a minimal pair, for contrast in minimal pairs is merely a heuristic for discovering a more fundamental contrast. This more fundamental contrast is contrast in system. A system in the sense being used here, is a set of language units which differ from each other along a certain finite set of parameters. In the grammatical hierarchy, the units are syntagmemes and the parameters of each field are expressible in terms of grammatical functions.

Though this last statement is not made overtly in statements of tagmemic theory, it can be shown to be consistent with the practice of tagmemicists. On the one hand, no tagmemic grammar, as far as I know, has posited two contrasting syntagmemes solely on the basis of differences in form. While it is true in a number of cases that the differences in form may be the most obvious differences, tagmemicists have always intuitively felt that a difference in grammatical relationship also existed. Thus, one might find in the description of a language two clause syntagmemes described as follows:[6]

A)Transitive clause = + Subject: NP + Predicate: VP_{-be} + Object: NP.
B) Equative clause = + Topic: NP + Predicate $_{Link}$: VP_{be} + Comp: NP.

The primary formal difference between A) and B) lies in the fact that the filler of the predicate in A) is all verbs other than *be*, while the filler of the predicate in B) is the verb *be*. But this is not the only difference posited between the two clauses. Differences in functions are posited as well. The second NP in A), for example, fills the object function while the second NP in B) fills the complement function. Such a situation is typical of tagmemic practice.

A second bit of evidence that the parameters of grammatical fields are grammatical functions arises from the fact that in all cases which I have examined in which an author has attempted to present a system of contrasting syntagmemes, differences in the component functions are the parameters of the system. A typical case in point is the following matrix adapted from Liem (1966) showing a portion of the system of English clauses.

Each cell in every row has some set of functions (or absence of functions) in common and each cell in every column has some set of functions (or absence of functions) in common.

A level is a system of contrasting syntagmemes. A hierarchy is a system of contrasting levels. These two definitions in conjunction with what has already been said about system (in particular that the parameters of a system are definable in terms of surface structure function),imply that the various levels within a hierarchy are to be contrasted and identified by the various functional relations posited for the syntagmemes with each level.

That is, roughly, a clause is a clause because it contains a predicate-like

INDEPENDENT CLAUSES

	Declarative Clause	Imperative Clause	Yes-No Interrogative Clause
Intransitive	+ S + Act Intr Decl Pr He ran.	+Act Intr Imp Pr Run!	+ S + Act Intr Inter Pr Did he run?
Single Transitive	+ S + Act Sg Tr Decl Pr + DO She guided the tourists.	+ Act Sg Tr Imp Pr + DO Guide the tourists!	+ S + Act Sg Tr Inter Pr + DO Did she guide the tourists?
Double Transitive	+ S + Act Db Tr Decl Pr + IO + DO They gave John a book	+ Act Db Tr Imp Pr + IO + DO Give John a book!	+ S + Act Db Tr Inter Pr + IO + DO Did they give John a book?
Attributive Transitive	+ S + Act At Tr Decl Pr + DO + At They selected him chairman	+ Act At Tr Imp Pr + DO + At Elect him chairman!	+ S + Act At Tr Inter Pr + DO + At Did they select him Chairman?
Equational	+ S + Eq Decl Pr + Eq Co She was kind.	+ Eq Imp Pr + Eq Co Be kind!	+ S + Eq Inter Pr + Eq Co Is she kind?

8

tagmeme while a phrase is a phrase because it contains tagmemes such as head, modifier, etc. It is worth noting here that in saying this I am merely emphasizing one aspect of the definition of levels, especially the clause and phrase levels already used by tagmemicists. Thus, in Elson and Picket, the definition of clause included the statement

> A clause construction is any string of tagmemes which consists of or includes one and only one predicate or predicate-like tagmeme among the constituent tagmemes of the string... (1962:64)

Similarly, Longacre included the following sentence in his definition of phrase.

> [A phrase] may be single centered, double centered, or relator-axis; and expresses such relationships as head-modifier, linkage of elements, or relation of an element to the clause by means of an overt relator (1964:74).

These two statements are examples of the type of statement advocated here. The difficulties with them lie in the fact that the first statement is over-simple, since there are constructions which we may want to call clauses, but which do not contain predicate or predicate-like constructions. Note, for instance, the following examples:

a) *(I don't like) John playing near the railing.*
b) *With the king safely out of the way, (the barons quickly distributed among themselves the wealth of the commoners).*
c) *(I wanted) John to come.*

Longacre's statement is more complete, but does not seem to be unified by any underlying principle. One could justifiably ask whether these relations have anything in common which contrast them as a group with relations which are typical of clauses or words. This question can best be answered by relating the various levels to the functions they play within connected discourse. Pike and Pike (unpublished) attempt to do this, I believe, by classifying levels according to their communication load. They set up five types of communications load: social interaction, theme development, proposition, term, and lexical package (Chapter 3). Although it is not entirely clear from their discussion, these communication loads seem to be aspects of meaning which are provided by the surface grammatical form. In other words, if an idea is encoded as a clause or a sentence, it is a proposition, while if the same idea is encoded as a sequence of sentences, it constitutes a theme development. Thus we can have a single situation, encoded first as a simple clause, then as a sequence of sentences uttered by one person, and last as a sequence of sentences uttered by two people.

I. *The child in the water really surprised Mary by splashing her.*
II. *The child was in the water. He really surprised Mary by splashing her.*
III. Abe: *The child was in the water.*
Bill: *Yeah, and he really surprised Mary by splashing her.*

Even though the situation described by the language remains constant, the first example is a proposition, the second a theme development, and the third a social interaction.[7] The following chart adapted from Pike and Pike (unpublished) shows the relation between the various communication loads and the grammatical units which encode them.

Communication Load	Grammatical Level	
	Minimum	Maximum
social interaction	exchange	conversation
theme development	paragraph	monologue
proposition	clause	sentence
term	word	phrase
lexical package	morpheme	stem

(Pike and Pike, Chapter 3)

As is evident from the chart, this approach to the definition of levels results in a pairing of grammatical levels. Both members of each pair of levels have the same communicative load, but one level consists of the minimum grammatical units which can convey that load, while the other member of the pair consists of expanded units which convey that load. Thus both phrases and words encode terms in a proposition. Phrases may be considered to be (roughly) sequences of words; in other words, an expanded unit consisting of words and closely related to words. Similarly, both clauses and sentences encode propositions, with sentences consisting of clauses and modifiers of clauses. Each of the ten grammatical levels mentioned in the chart differs structurally from every other level. The causes of the structural differences are of two types. Each pair differs from every other pair because of the communication load, while the members of each pair differ as to expansion possibilities. Words and phrases have the structures they do in order to encode terms (either simply or in a more complex manner). (See also the discussion of these levels by K.L. Pike in the last chapter of this volume.)

Of the communication loads named above, perhaps the most important is that of social interaction, for this is one of the major functions of language. It is not surprising, therefore, to find the Pikes using the concept of social interaction (two people interacting via language) to define some of the basic concepts of language. In particular they use minimal units of language which can initiate conversations.

Given an exchange (a minimum dialog) (and assuming that we can recognise and for the moment eliminate attention to greeting forms, calls, exclamations, and other standard-ized, stereotyped bits), we will say that a *minimum initiating speech* is an *independent clause*, that the *minimum reply* is a *word*; and that such an independant clause is simultaneously an *independent sentence*, whereas a word filling the reply slot is a *dependent sentence*. Thus word, clause, and sentence are in their first definition tied to the exchange level of the hierarchy. (Pike and Pike, chapter 3)

I suspect that the Pikes have left out an intermediate step in their reasoning here, and that the definitions above will be seen to be integrated within the system if we make this step explicit. In particular, it seems to me that they ignore the role of proposition and term in this system. To integrate these terms into the system they need only say that a minimum initiating speech in a conversation must convey a complete proposition. The minimum structure which conveys a complete proposition is an independent clause (which is a minimum independent sentence). Similarly, a minimum reply in a conver-sation need only overtly encode part of a proposition, a term. The minimum structure which encodes a term is a word. Hence words may be used as minimum replies in a conversation. But these minimum replies are understood in a conversation with reference to the way they relate to what has gone on before. In other words, even though they overtly encode only a portion of a proposition, they are understood as if they encoded a complete proposition. For this reason, then, we can say that words which are minimum replies in a conversation are dependent sentences.

SECTION III

During the 1950's and 1960's most of the effort of tagmemicists was directed toward the development of the theory just presented. Another aspect of language largely unexplored during this time, was the semantic aspect of language. This is not to say that tagmemicists were at any time uninterested in language as a means of expressing meaning. In fact, because of their practical reasons for being interested in language at all, they were and are deeply interested in the use of language to express meaning. The problem lay in the integration of meaning into tagmemic theory in a motivated and satisfying way. One can see Pike struggling with this problem in 1954 when he considers examples such as *John runs home. John has been hit in the eye. John was given the man,* and *John is the teacher,* and concludes

at least some of these sentences must be considered as beginning with separate tagmemes because of the sharp differences in their structural meaning and proportion (...e.g. actor-as-subject, versus recipient-of-action as subject)... (Pike [1954] 1967:246)

Ten years later, when revising his work, Pike returned to this problem and tried

to follow the flow of dramatis personae, and of other situational roles of the real world... through a discourse. (Pike 1967:246 fn 14.)

He found this difficult to do with traditional tagmemic notation since items which filled essentially the same grammatical functions were often quite different with respect to their role in the real-world situation being described. Similarly, items which had similar roles in the real world often appeared in radically different grammatical guises. As a result, he was forced to return to the actor-as-subject concept, and develop a notation which kept track of both the grammatical function and the real-world role. The approach he takes in 1964 differs from the earlier approach in that in the earlier discussion he suggests that it is necessary for the proper description of English clauses to distinguish between actor-as-subject and recipient-of-action as subject, while in the later discussion he makes a similar proposal in order to account for the structure of a discourse.

We have attempted to show the practical and theoretical advantages of relating two components of language structure:
On the one hand, discourse structure requires for its study techniques by which one can recognize continuity of individual situational invariants – situational roles – as they migrate through the structure. On the other hand, these elements representing situations in the real world find themselves garbed in different dress; they appear in various grammatical roles and are represented by differing lexical items. Therefore the study of discourse structure must be supplemented by a study of tagmeme structure represented in a way which allows one to see both the grammatical role and the invariant situational role. (Pike 1964:18)

In this article he sets one of the goals of tagmemic theory.

...ideally... one should be able to develop an etics of tagmeme display such that dimensions of situation and grammatical role can be presented so that one has easilly available a summary of tagma types which have been discovered around the world and which are available for recognition and treatment. (1964:18)

This has been a major thrust in the development of tagmemic theory since. Things were not always easy. It took Fillmore's development of case grammar published in 1966 and 1968 to show once and for all that situational roles were indeed necessary to the description of grammatical constructions and to provide a means for systematizing these phenomena. Once these works were available tagmemicists seized case grammar and began to integrate it into their theory. In 1967 Becker studied conjoining and the English subject tagmeme and found he had to treat cases such as performer and undergoer along with grammatical functions (subject, object) grammatical classes (NP, VP, Prep Ph.) and also features of words (male, animate, human). After Becker's work a series of dissertations and articles have appeared using derivatives of Fillmorean case grammar as part of the theoretical underpinning. (See, for example, Wise 1971 (originally 1968); Platt 1971 (originally 1970); Cook 1971, 1972.)

It soon became evident that Fillmorean case grammar was not quite exactly what tagmemicists needed. The most obvious problem was that it was not extensive enough for the purposes of tagmemicists. Fillmorean case grammar dealt only with relations between participants in a predication. This was certainly useful, but tagmemicists, with their interest in analyzing discourse also needed to deal with relations between predications and between groups of predications. This entailed a relatively straightforward extension of case grammar, and it is in this sense that one must understand Longacre's four calculi: predicate calculus (essentially case grammar), statement calculus (deals with possible relations between propositions), calculus of repartee, and increment calculus. Each of these calculi is intended to describe meanings which are typically (but not exclusively) realized by one level of grammatical structure. As a result, I suspect that more calculi will be needed to account for the semantics of phrase level and word level constructions. While not all tagmemicists talk about calculi, nor do they all have as elaborate a system as Longacre, they do have much the same sort of system to deal with this aspect of language. (For examples, see Pike-Pike 1974; Trail 1973; Cook 1971, 1972; Wise 1971; Hale 1973a, 1973b.)

The second objection to Fillmorean case grammar related more directly to the nature of case grammar and its role within tagmemic theory. Two aspects of this objection are described by Austin Hale. First,

Fillmorean cases appeared to incorporate a great deal which is, from our point of view, non-relational. The feature of animateness was a part of the definition of certain cases.

From our point of view the specification of animateness belonged to[another part of the grammar], and we did not wish to treat it again as part of the definition of a sememic relationship. We wished, for example, to be able to show parallelisms between the sememic relationships of subject to verb (or to clause) in examples such as the following:
14. The river washed the boulder away with a sudden torrent of water.
15. John scrubbed the dirt away with a brush.
16. The locomotive cleared the snow away with the snowplough.
In some sense, *the river, John,* and *the locomotive* are all actors and are in some sense capable of the actions named by their accompanying verbs. Yet neither the river nor the locomotive is animate in the sense of a volitional responsible initiator and neither is personified in these instances. If these could not be agents by virtue of their animateness, then we would need another case, say inanimate agent. (Hale 1973b: 5-6)

This objection has a second facet having to do with the sub-categorization of words. As Hale mentioned in the quotation given above, tagmemicists attempt to distinguish between relationships between words (and constructions) and the various (ideosyncratic) properties of individual words or sets of words. Hale remarks:

restrictions on the [Fillmorean] case relations a given word can enter into seem to have a great deal to do with what a given word means. This we found uncomfortable. (Hale 1973b: 7)

The third objection tagmemicists had to Fillmorean case grammar was that Fillmore did not distinguish between case realizations which occur within the nucleus of the clause and those which occur within the margin. Indeed, it would have been surprising had he done so, considering the fact that transformational grammar, the model that he was using, makes no allowance for such a distinction. In setting up a taxonomy of clause types, tagmemicists find it more useful to keep track of participants which are realized in the nucleus of a clause than those which are realized in the margin. It is felt that those are the ones which are most useful in subcategorizing predicates.

Constituents that were optional and whose optional occurence possibility could be predicted in terms of other items in the clause were tentatively excluded from the clause nucleus. (Hale 1973b: 7)

This implies that such constituents were excluded from consideration.
If we turn to a positive vein, the tagmemic description of the lexemic aspect of a construction will include a description of the semantic relations which hold between the various parts of that construction. (If the construction is a clause, then the semantic relations will be roles which are purely relational rather than combining relations with the properties of the fillers of the roles.) In addition to the relations which hold between the various portions of the construction the grammar must specify categorial information

14

relevant to each of the fillers of the semantic relations. Here we would expect
to find distinctions such as animate vs. inanimate or human vs. non-human
when dealing with nouns, action vs. state when dealing with verbs, and
perhaps, count vs. mass when dealing with noun phrases,[8] And finally, the
grammar must give information about the particular referent of the
construction in context. If, in a story, one reads *The boy went home*, the
grammar must be able to indicate whether the referent of *the boy* has been
mentioned before, and if so, in which sentence.[9] In the remainder of this
section of this chapter I hope to sketch in the outlines of the relations and
features which tagmemicists have found necessary for their description of
language. While the major outlines of these facets of language are pretty well
agreed on, there is enough disagreement about the specific analyses to make it
impossible to give a neat coherent summary which will represent all positions.
As a result, I will confine myself to presenting the system used by one
individual for each level.

In describing propositions, Pike and Pike (unpublished) find it necessary
to distinguish between actions and states. Though they do not describe this
distinction, the examples they give show that they are using the distinction
presented in current linguistic literature. (See Lakoff 1970: 121f and Quirk
et al 1972 section 2.6 for examples). They depart from usual terminology by
referring to this distinction as a role distinction.

represented by the proposition (especially through its predicate...) (Pike-Pike,
unpublished chapter 4).

If there is no "action role" then the proposition is a state. They need in
addition to this distinction four other roles; actor, undergoer, scope, and
complement.[10] The actor is the participant which performs the action or is in
the state referred to by the predicate. In contrast with Fillmore's Agent, it is
not required that the actor be animate, thus among the examples they cite
are:

A   U   Sc
The wind swept the pictures off the wall.
A   U   Sc
The trees took moisture from the ground.
A   Sc
Abe is in his office.
A   U
He owned three cars.

A   U

I wanted a dog.

Note that the first two examples are action predications (the proposition contains an action role) while the last three examples are state predications (the proposition contains no action role.)

    The undergoer is the participant which receives the action of the verb. (See examples above). Complement occurs when there is "a second (non-reflexive) reference to some nuclear participant" (Pike and Pike, unpublished, Chapter

        A   Co   A   Co

4). Thus in *John is tall* and *John is a teacher, tall,* and *a teacher* are complements. "Scope is defined negatively, as a participant relation which is neither actor or undergoer" (Pike-Pike, unpublished, Chaper 4). (I would add that scope is also not a complement.) The fact that it is defined negatively allows considerable range to the types of relations which may be included within it. It will include everything from person to location.

    The following examples will give a feeling for its range.

A   Sc   A   Sc U   A   U
Mary left the house. He handed me the tools. He put both hands

Sc   Sc   Co Sc   U
on the rudder. She turned 75. The car needed new tires.

Once these role relations are established as variables which account for differences between predications, it is possible to arrive at an etic classification of all clauses. (See *idem* for further discussion.)

    Turning now to relations between propositions we find that several tagmemicists have developed taxonomies of the relations which may hold between propositions. Ballard-Conrad-Longacre 1971a, 1971b present a relatively elaborate taxonomy of these relations. (Longacre 1972 presents a slightly revised version of this taxonomy.) Trail (1973) and Pike and Pike (unpublished) present simpler taxonomies. The difference in the taxonomies result, I believe, from a difference in opinion as to whether the categorial information about the specific propositions involved in a general relationship will be sufficient to account for a particular sub meaning of that relation.

    I present here pp. 16-17 a chart from Trail (1973) which lists the relations between propositions which he feels are necessary to account for the sentences he has treated.

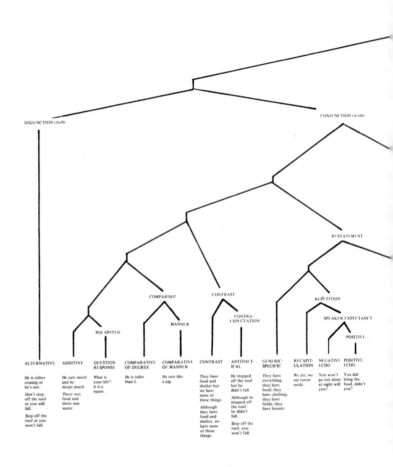

17

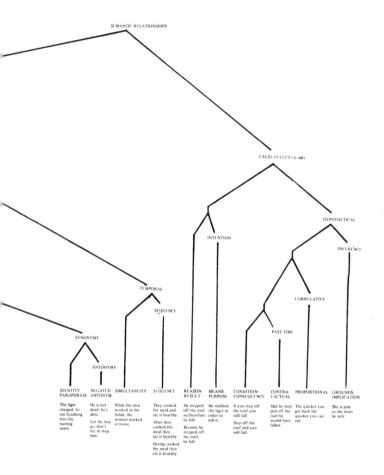

SEMANTIC RELATIONSHIPS

CAUSE-EFFECT (A→B)

HYPOTHETICAL

INTENTION

INFERENCE

TEMPORAL

CORRELATIVE

SEQUENCE

SYNONYMY

PAST TIME

ANTONYMY

IDENTITY PARAPHRASE	NEGATED ANTONYM	SIMULTANEITY	SEQUENCE	REASON-RESULT	MEANS-PURPOSE	CONDITION-CONSEQUENCE	CONTRA-FACTUAL	PROPORTIONAL	GROUNDS-IMPLICATION
The tiger charged; he ran headlong into the waiting snare.	He is not dead; he's alive. Let the boy go, don't try to stop him.	While the men worked in the fields, the women worked at home.	They cooked the meal and ate it heartily. After they cooked the meal they ate it heartily. Having cooked the meal they ate it heartily.	He stepped off the roof so/therefore he fell. Because he stepped off the roof, he fell.	He stabbed the tiger in order to kill it.	If you step off the roof you will fall. Step off the roof and you will fall.	Had he stepped off the roof he would have fallen.	The quicker you get back the quicker you can eat.	She is pale so she must be sick.

18

When one compares the chart of semantic relations given above with the
following chart's (from Longacre 1970, p. 784) description of the surface
level

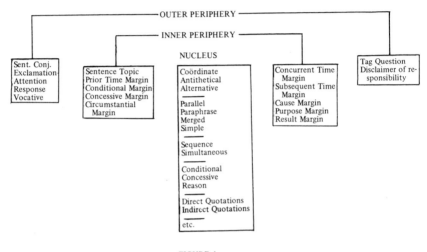

FIGURE 1

(1) Linear order on the chart is intended to reflect a statistically common ordering among the world's languages.
(2) Outer Periphery items permute to grammatical junctures within Inner Periphery and Nucleus in many languages.
(3) Nuclear sentence strings may occur recursively within the Inner Periphery and the Nucleus.
(4) A perticle such as English *then* intervenes in many languages between certain preposed Sentence Margins and
the Nucleus.
(5) In the Outer Periphery, the symbol 'Sent. Conj.' stands for a set of positions, such as SENTENCE CONJUNC-
TION, SENTENCE ADVERB, and SENTENCE MODIFIER, e.g. *and, nevertheless, obviously...*

grammatical structure typical of sentences around the world, one finds that a
number of structures are not accounted for. Some of these, such as attention
(*Hey, the chair's here*), vocative (*John, the chair's here*), and response (*Yes,
the chair's here*) will best be dealt with on the next higher level when
meanings involving the interaction of two people are dealt with. (See the
chapter in this series by Longacre.) This cannot be said for the meanings of
other structures (sentence modifiers, for example). In the sentence *Maybe he
came early*, the relation of *maybe* to the rest of the sentence does not seem to
be similar to any of the types of relations discussed so far. In other words, a

new group of relations must be explored, this one having to do with modalities of the truth value of the proposition given by the sentence.

One possible candidate for this set of relations is the increment calculus proposed by Longacre (1972:81-86). One difficulty with this proposal is that Longacre says he sets up his increment calculus to deal specifically with structures involving two verbs, an auxiliary and a verb, or a verb and certain types of affixes. That is to say, the primary reason he cites for proposing a new category of meanings is how they get expressed. Thus, in discussing the motivation for proposing increment calculus as a separate type of deep structure relation, he says:

I am speaking here of certain specialized two-base structures, the purpose of which is to express in one or the other of the bases such relations as Direction (go, come), Desire (want to), Intent (intend to), Ability (can, can't), Obligation (should, must, ought to), and Causation (make someone do something). The base containing such a verb acts in many ways like an auxiliary or modal – into which such structures sometimes historically develop... it is so common among the world's languages to express such things as Direction, Desire, etc. as either affixes on a verb, particles in the verb phrase, or auxiliary verbs, that we would do well to posit a further deep structure level to accomodate these surface structure elements. (Longacre 1972:81)

In the discussion which follows this passage, however, Longacre gives a number of examples in which several of the meanings (e.g. Duration and Modality) are expressed by combinations of sentences. In other words, the essential point that he is making is that there are a number of meanings which differ radically from the meanings treated by all other levels of deep structure. I would add that these meanings may be expressed in a number of ways in languages around the world. If we look just at the various ways in which English expresses modalities of a proposition, we can find at least the following range.

1) modal – *He may come.*
2) independent verb – *He happened to come.*
3) clause-level modifier – *He came by chance.*
4) sentence-level modifier – *Maybe be came.*[11]
5) parenthetical expressions (as afterthought) – *He came early, I think.*[12]

All of the expressions cited above seem to convey meanings which are quite similar and hence probably constitute a single system of meaning contrasts. Halliday (1970) attempts to integrate the meanings expressed by the English modals and by adverbs such as *perhaps, maybe*, and *possibly*, into a single semantic system. Perhaps tagmemicists in their exploration of this aspect of meaning will be able to extend his work to apply to their needs.[13]

Since their interest has been focussed on relations between larger units, tagmemicists have had little time to explore the semantic relations which hold between the constituents of phrases. These relations are not simple, and any attempt to describe them in this chapter can be regarded only as a preliminary exploration of the problem rather than a coherent presentation of a semantic system (which we might call, following Longacre's model, 'participant calculus'). Since I am most familiar with the English noun phrase (see Fries 1970), I will use that construction as the source of my examples.

One is tempted to say that noun phrases may be analyzed semantically as containing a referent which has the various properties expressed by the head noun and the various words modifying the head noun. In this way, the phrase *old men who snore* would be analyzed as a referent x which has the properties 'men', 'old' and 'x snore'. It is quickly seen, however, that this cannot account for the use of the articles since these do not express a property. Similarly we cannot account for the meaning of the last noun phrase of *Bill read few books that were interesting* by saying that that noun phrase has a referent x which has the attributes 'few', 'book', and 'x were interesting' since that analysis would imply that Bill read few books. This clearly does not have to be the case. The original sentence says that of the books that Bill read (however many that was), few were interesting. In other words, words such as *few, several, twenty,* etc., cannot be considered to express slightly strange attributes which are then added to the attributes expressed in other portions of the noun phrase, with the total meaning of the noun phrase expressed as a concatenation of all the attributes expressed by the various words and constructions within the noun phrase. These words must instead relate directly to the referent of the noun phrase independent of the attributes expressed elsewhere in the phrase. Thus, a more satisfying description of the noun phrase above would be 'few x such that x were[14] books and x were interesting.'

This approach to the description of the meaning of indefinite numerals will in fact hold for the description of the meaning contribution of the whole determiner system. The article *the,* for example, indicates that the referent of the noun phrase is known to the listener/reader from linguistic, social, or situational context. Thus the last noun phrase in the sentence *John read the book on trigonometry.* would be analyzed as 'a known x, such that x is a book and x is on trigonometry'. (The word *the*, of course, does not say why the listener knows the referent.).[15]

When we turn to a more complete analysis of the modifiers in the noun phrase we find that a simple additive model of semantic contribution will not work here either. One frequently finds modifiers which do not express attributes of the referent, but rather modify the reference of the noun phrase.

Following Bolinger (1967: 20) I call the first type of modification
referent modification and the second type *reference modification*. Modifiers
which express referent modification are additive; modifiers which express
reference modification are not additive. The modifiers which express referent
modificat:on include all relative clauses, postnominal modifiers which are
derived from relative clauses, and certain loose knit modifiers. Thus, *that old
picture on the wall by the door* could be analyzed as having the following
meaning. 'That (pointing) x such that x is a picture, x is old, x is on the wall,
and x is by the door.[16]

Compare the analysis of that phrase with the analysis of *a true thermoplastic*. It would be wrong to say that this phrase means 'x such that x is a
thermoplastic and x is true'. We must rather say that *true* is an intensifier of
thermoplastic. As an intensifier it does not relate directly to the referent of
the noun phrase, but rather modifies the reference of the head. In a sense *true*
resembles a modality on a proposition in that it qualifies the degree to which
the referent possesses the attributes expressed by the noun phrase. Thus *a
true thermoplastic* possesses all the essential attributes of thermoplastics,
while *a virtual thermoplastic* possesses most of these attributes but not all.
Similarly *an accused murderer* is not yet a *murderer*, and *a putative example*
of something is not really an example of that thing.[17] Apparently these
modalities may apply to only a portion of the noun phrase. A newscaster
reported once that a person had "suffered an apparent fatal heart attack". It
was clear that the man was dead so the modality could only apply to the
cause of death. That is to say, the description of the meaning of this phrase
would not read 'x such that x is an apparently (fatal heart attack)' but rather
'x such that x is an apparent (heart attack) and x was fatal'. Similarly *a virtual
three-way tie* is not virtually three way, but virtually a tie (involving three
teams).

If we ask what sorts of meanings are expressed by the two types of
modifiers we find the following situation. In each case of referent modification, the modifier is either a complete predication (if it is a relative clause)
or it can be the subject complement of a clause with the main verb *be*. If we
compare the meanings expressed by these modifiers with the meanings which
we have described above for predications, we find that these modifiers
express either the whole predication or the role of complement. In other
words, the meanings expressed by referent modifiers are totally accounted for
by the relations expressed within a proposition.

This is not the case with modifiers which express reference modification.
In no case may a complete proposition be used to modify the reference of a
noun phrase, nor have I found any instance of reference modification
expressing the proposition-level role of complement. Almost any other

propositional role may be so expressed, however, and even a number of relations which typically hold between propositions may be found within noun phrases. Thus we find reference modification expressed by Loose-Knit modifiers indicating time and manner (*his former wife, a beautiful dancer* ('she dances beautifully', not 'she is beautiful'). Considerably more variety is found within the Close-Knit modifier. Almost any proposition level role may be expressed by a Close-Knit modifier: actor, *Viking carvings of human heads*; undergoer, *voltage measurements*; time, *the 1959 crisis*; location, *the Indochina war*. In addition to these relations we find measure (*a two story building, a two pound fish*), purpose *(operating margins, a road tax, an airborne navigation system)*, and two types of partitive relations. In the first the modifier indicates a particular unit while the total noun phrase refers to a part of that unit (*the pool bottom, the sentence end*) while in the other the modifier indicates a unit or substance while the total noun phrase indicates a portion (*a carrot cube, a cloth fragments*, or *a dance suite, a measurement program*.)[18]

Two last points must be made before we leave the description of the relations which hold within noun phrases. First, it seems possible to have (at least implied) time restrictions on the attribute applied to the referent of the noun phrase. To say, for example, *Mary is looking for a husband* does not necessarilly imply that she is intent on breaking up a marriage. That is she is not necessarily looking for a man who is already married, but rather she is looking for a man who will be a husband to her. Similarly, to say that *That old man led the charge forty years ago* does not imply that he was old when he led the charge nor does the sentence *The king took as hostage an infant whom twenty years later he married* imply that the king married an infant. It is true that adjectives like *old* and *young* and nouns like *infant* and *boy* have the concept of time within their definitions, so in these cases we should expect limitations with respect to when these attributes are to be applied to the referent. In the case of the word *husband* however, the concept of time is not a part of the definition of the word, hence we will probably need some method of making such restrictions explicit.

The last problem which we will discuss here is the fact that some noun phrases do not seem to have the same sort of reference that other noun phrases have. The sentence *Bill is a diplomat*, for example, is ambiguous. It may be interpreted to mean that Bill is a member of the diplomatic corps, that is to say, Bill·belongs to the class 'diplomat'. The other interpretation, the one which is relevant here, is that Bill possesses some of the attributes necessary to being a good diplomat. In this interpretation *a diplomat*, is to be interpreted very much like an adjective. Thus one does not need to be a member of the diplomatic corps to be a diplomat in this sense. We can, therefore, truthfully say *that three year old is a diplomat*. In fact, this sentence is very close in meaning to *That three year old is diplomatic*. The adjectival character of *a diplomat* in this sentence becomes even more obvious when one realizes that nouns in this function may be graded. (*Bill is a real diplomat. Bill is more of a diplomat than John is. Bill is more diplomat than general.*)[19]

Two more topics remain in our discussion of the lexemic aspect of language. These are the categorical information relevant to each of the fillers of the semantic relations, and information about the referent of a particular construction in the context in which it occurs. In fact, it will be impossible to do more than assert that these aspects of language must be dealt with and sketch the sorts of phenomena which might be found. The categorical information relevant to each of the fillers of the semantic relations will include semantic features such as animate-inanimate, human-nonhuman, singular-plural, etc. Transformational grammarians long ago pointed out that the inclusion of such features was essential if we were to account for the grammar of a language. Thus in order to determine whether to use *who* or *which* as a relative pronoun one has to determine whether the words which or who are referring to the head of the noun phrase which is a human noun or a non-human noun. This example illustrates both the strength of this approach and its weakness. First it is clear that if we are to avoid phrases like **the boy which came* and **the letter who came* we must refer to information of this sort. On the other hand, this analysis implies that each word is classified as either human or non-human, animate or inanimate, etc. Tagmemicists feel that these attributes are not attributes of the words, but rather attributes of the referents of the words. How else can one account for the possibility of both *the group which came* and *the group who came*, and the fact that the occurrence of *which* and *who* is determined by the reference of *group*. If *group* refers to a group of books, then *which* must be used. If *group* refers to people (thought of individually) then *who* is likely to be used, while if *group* refers to people (not thought of individually) then *which* is likely to be used..

An interesting implication of the approach tagmemicists are taking to this problem is that their model forces them to assign features to every unit they treat. Thus, not only will nouns, verbs and adjectives have features, but also noun phrases, prepositional phrases, clauses, and sentences will have features analogous to these. Little work has been done to explore what these features might be, so it is impossible to evaluate this proposal at the present time. One can only say that proposals similar to this have occasionally been made on a much smaller scale. In 1966, for example, Weinreich made a persuasive argument that the feature [count] be considered "a feature of the noun phrase as a whole" (p. 436). He thus introduced the possibility that

24

constructions might introduce features, but this position is very far from requiring that every construction introduce some features.

Finally we may turn to the specification of the reference of the particular morphemes and words which realize a particular function. It is obvious that in order to understand a story one must be able to keep track of who is doing what. In other words, one must keep track of the referents of the various constructions. There are, however, some more obviously grammatical structures which can only be interpreted if one keeps track of the referents. One case in point is the interpretation of reflexive pronouns. These, whether they fill a clause level function (*Bill paid himself first*) or serve a kind of intensifying function (*The teacher couldn't solve the problem himself*), indicate that the referent of the reflexive is the same as the referent of some other phrase within the clause. Similarly, to interpret a relative clause within a noun phrase we must know that the referent of the relative pronoun is the same as the referent of the total noun phrase. Thus the phrase *many men who like chicken* is to be interpreted as 'many x such that x are men and x like chicken' (where the referent of the total noun phrase x recurs as a portion of the relative clause).[20]

SECTION IV

We have now described surface structure and we have described a lexemic structure; we must now deal with the relation between the two. It is worthwhile to emphasize again that Pike and a number of other tagmemicists would object to the separation of surface und underlying structure, while Longacre tends to allow more of a separation. I have no examples of any cases in which this attitude leads Longacre inevitably to conclusions which Pike would reject. It is, however, a significant difference in point of view and may lead to just such a difference.

Both Pike and Longacre work with the notion of a normal relationship between underlying structure and surface structure, and both allow various departures from the norm of specific reasons. Both claim that both underlying and surface structures are essential to the description of language. We can point to the description of conjunction to illustrate this necessity. One cannot conjoin two units which do not fill the same surface grammatical function. One can say, for example, *imperial and provincial control of trade*, or *the emperor's and the provinces' control of trade*, but one cannot conjoin one from one phrase and one from the other, e.g. **the emperor's and provincial control of trade*. Note that the ungrammaticality here has little to do with identity of *form*. It is quite possible to conjoin two items which do not belong to the same class, provided they fill the same function and role, e.g. *State and federal control of trade*.

On the other hand one cannot conjoin two units which do not fill the same lexemic role. Thus one can paraphrase *John supported his mother* as either *John's support (got her through)* or *His mother's support (was an awful burden)*. But though both *John's* and *his mother's* fill the same grammatical function (Determiner 2) we cannot conjoin the two and get *John's and his mother's support* as a nominalization of the original clause.

Pike's approach to the problem of describing all the various aspects of language is to stick by his definition of unit as a close association of form and meaning. Since form has two aspects, grammatical form and phonological form, he is required by his approach to give three major aspects of each unit; the grammatical form, the lexemic interpretation, and the phonological form. But within each of these three aspects of language there are three types of information which must be supplied; information about functions, information about the filler classes, and information about the specific items which are used in a particular expression. Thus we must give nine types of information about any unit we describe.

	Function	Filler Class	Specific Item
Grammatical	1	2	3
Lexemic	4	5	6
Phonological	7	8	9

The phonological aspect (the three boxes in the lower row) have not been explored at all within this framework and will be ignored in the remainder of this chapter — leaving six boxes. (Indeed the remainder of this chapter will focus on boxes, 1, 2, 4 and 5.)

Thus the transitive clause *The boy ate the bread* occurring in a text might be described in the following way:

1) It consists of a subject followed by a predicate followed by a direct object.
2) It consists of a noun phrase followed by a verb phrase followed by a noun phrase.
3) It consists of the morphemes *the, boy, past, eat, the, bread*.
4) It contains the roles actor, predication, undergoer.
5) The first noun phrase is an animate, count noun phrase...
The second noun phrase is an inanimate, mass noun phrase...

The verb is an eventive...

6) The referent of the first noun phrase is the referent which is mentioned in previous sentences as *Johnnie, John Smith III, young man,* (etc.).
This act of eating has not been referred to before in this text.
The referent of *the bread* was referred to as *a loaf of bread, slices of bread*
This information may be entered on the matrix in the following way:

Subj	Pred	D. Obj	NP	VP	NP	the + boy	past + eat	the bread
Actor	Predication		animate count	event past	inanimate mass	Ref x	event y	Ref z
	undergoer							

It should be obvious from the matrix given above that the matrix itself can be split up should that be convenient. In this case each tagmeme receives an individual matrix. It should be emphasized that this is merely a notational variant, and does not involve a significant change in the information presented.

	Subj	NP	the + boy
+	actor	animate	Ref X

	Pred	VP	past + eat
+	Predication	event	event y

	D. Obj	NP	the + bread
+	undergoer	inanimate mass	Ref Z

This approach assumes that there is a normal, or typical, association between the various boxes of the display and that if this association is changed, a new tagmeme results. This approach is illustrated by Pike and Pike's (developing an idea of Hale's) taxonomy of clause types based on the interaction of surface structure grammatical structures and participant roles. They abandon the usual classification of clause types on the basis of the presence or absence of structures such as direct object, indirect object, complement, etc, and substitute a classification based on those participant roles which are realized within the nucleus of the clause. Pike and Pike (unpublished, chapter 4) work with four participant roles: action, actor, undergoer and scope,[21] each of which may or may not occur. This gives a total of sixteen clause types which they describe in the chart (invented by A. Hale) on pp. 28-29.

Given this taxonomy one can study the interaction of the various boxes in the six box notation by noting the various forms which may be used to express a given idea. The forms[22] which will be allowed seem to be determined by 1) the particular verb in the predicate (box 3), 2) the meaning of that verb (box 6), and 3) the meanings of various complements (box 6, but of a tagmeme other than the predicate). Compare the following paradigms for three uses of the verb *wash*.

I.
i.   John washed the glue out of the shirts (with soap and water
       and a lot of elbow grease.)
ii.   *John washed the glue.
iii.   *The glue washed well.
iv.   The glue washed out of the shirts (very nicely).
v.   The glue was washed out of the shirts.
vi.   The glue was washed out of the shirts by John.
vii.   *The glue was washed by John.
viii. John washed the shirts.
ix.   *John washed the shirts of glue.
x.   John washed.
xi.   The shirts washed really nicely.
xii.   *The shirts washed of glue really nicely.
xiii. The shirts were washed.
xiv.   The shirts were washed by John.
xv.   *The shirts were washed of glue by John.

If we change the sense of the verb *wash* by changing the actor to *the river* we find the following paradigm.

II.
i.   The river washed the dirt from the pool.
ii.   *The river washed the dirt.
iii.   *The dirt washed well.
iv.   The dirt washed from the pool (very nicely).
v.   The dirt was washed from the pool.
vi.   The dirt was washed from the pool by the river.
vii.   *The dirt was washed by the river.
viii. The river washed the pool.
ix.   The river washed the pool of dirt.

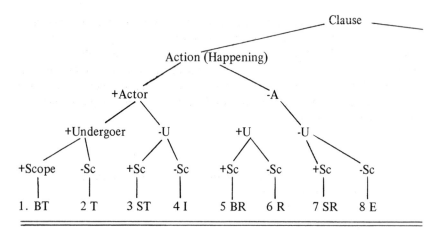

+Scope	-Sc	+Sc	-Sc	+Sc	-Sc	+Sc	-Sc
1. BT	2 T	3 ST	4 I	5 BR	6 R	7 SR	8 E

1. Action Bitransitive: ^A^He handed ^Sc^me the ^U^tools. ^A^He put ^U^both hands ^Sc^on the rudder. The ^A^wind swept the ^U^pictures ^Sc^off the wall. The ^A^trees took ^U^moisture ^Sc^from the ground. ^A^I emptied the ^U^water ^Sc^out-of the tank. ^A^Mary left₁ her ^U^purse ^Sc^home.

2. Action Transitive: That beautiful ^A^wave broke ^U^my collarbone. ^A^He learned the ^U^story. ^A^He got₁ (bought) a ^U^car.

3. Action Semitransitive: ^A^Mary left₂ ^Sc^the house. ^A^They went ^Sc^to town.

4. Action Intransitive: ^A^I chuckled. The ^A^wind howled. The ^A^wave broke (hitting on the beach).

5. Action Bireceptive: ^Sc^I broke ^U^my collarbone. The ^Sc^men received ^U^the prize. ^Sc^He got₂(received) a ^U^car. A ^U^car was given ^Sc^to him. ^Sc^He was given a ^U^car.

6. Action Receptive: ^U^My collarbone broke. The ^U^accident occurred (before our eyes). The ^U^butter melted. The ^U^stove got ^CO-^hot. Their ^U^supplies ran-out. ^U^My collarbone was broken (by the wave).

7. Action Semireceptive: ^Sc^She turned ^Co-^75. The ^Sc^liquid became ^Co-^gas.

8. Action Eventive: ^Ø^It rained. ^Ø^It got ^Co-^too hot.

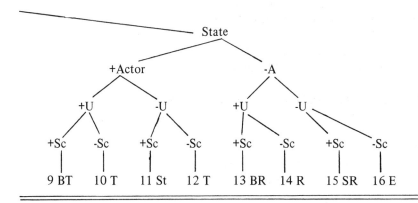

```
                                        State
                    +Actor                              -A
             +U            -U                   +U              -U
          +Sc   -Sc     +Sc    -Sc          +Sc    -Sc      +Sc      -Sc
           |     |       |      |            |      |         |        |
          9 BT  10 T    11 St  12 T        13 BR   14 R     15 SR    16 E
```

9. State Bitransitive: He had₂ both hands on the rudder. Someone owes him a medal. We keep the money in a box.

10. State Transitive: He knew the story. He had₁(owned) apples. I wanted the dog. The tree shaded the path.

11. State Semitransitive: Abe is in his office. Bill lives in New York.

12. State Intransitive: I felt foolish.

13. State Bireceptive: The box contained toys. The car needed new tires.

14. State Receptive: The path forked (at the big rock). The food tasted good (to me).

15. State Semireceptive: My collarbone is crooked. He is a singer. The figure resembles an owl.

16. State Eventive: It was rainy. It is too hot.

30

x.   *The river washed.
xi.   ? The pool washed really nicely
xii. *The pool washed of dirt really nicely.
xiii. ? The pool was washed.
xiv. ? The pool was washed by the river.
xv.   *The pool was washed of dirt by the river.

If we change the meaning of the adjunct from that of a source, (*from the pool*) to one of goal, (*down stream*), we find a third paradigm.

III.
i.   The river washed the dirt down stream.
ii.   *The river washed the dirt.
iii.   *The dirt washed well.
iv.   The dirt washed down stream.
v.   The dirt was washed down stream.
vi.   The dirt was washed down stream by the river.
vii.   *The dirt was washed by the river.
viii. *The river washed down stream.
ix.   *The river washed down stream (of) dirt.
x.   *The river washed.
xi.   *Down stream washed really nicely.
xii.   *Down stream washed (of) dirt really nicely.
xiii. *Down stream was washed (really nicely).
xiv.   *Down stream was washed by the river.
xv.   *Down stream was washed (of) dirt by the river.

These three paradigms have some interesting similarities and differences. First, they are similar in that they seem to fall into two parts: examples i-vii seem to focus on glue and dirt as the undergoer of the action, while examples viii-xv seem to focus on the shirts, the pool, and down stream as undergoer (with varying success). Thus sentence i seems to be analyzable in each case as parallel to Pike and Pike's example:

```
        A          U          Sc
        The wind swept the pictures off the wall.
        A          U      Sc
I-i     John washed the glue out of the shirts.
        A          U        Sc
II-i    The river washed the dirt from the pool.
```

```
        A          U      Sc
III-i   The river washed the dirt down stream.
```

Examples I-viii, and II-viii on the other hand seem to be analyzable parallel to
Pike and Pike's example[23]

```
        A          U
        He bought a car.
        A          U
I-viii  John washed the shirts.
        A              U
II-viii ? The river washed the pool.
```

In the case of *the glue* and *the dirt* (and *the pictures*) in examples i-vii, we
find the following restriction: These may not occur as subjects of either
active or passive sentences unless the scope is also expressed (see examples ii,
iii, and vii above). Since scopes are subject to this sort of restriction[24] we
ought to suspect that these words do not indicate the undergoer, but instead
indicate the scope.[25] If this is true, then the difference between examples
i-vii and viii-xv is not a difference in the participant roles the various
constituents play (as was suggested above) but rather a difference in the
surface grammatical manifestations of these roles.

When we turn to examples viii-xv we find that *the shirts, the pool,* and
down stream do not play the role of undergoer equally well. Indeed, *down
stream* cannot fill that role at all, while *the shirts* plays that role quite easily.
The fact that *the pool* is somewhat uncomfortable in this role in its example
sentences indicates that more is involved in this difference than the mere fact
that *down stream* is a prepositional phrase while *the shirts* is a noun phrase.
The interpretation of the verb *wash* in the various sentences also has
something to do with the acceptability of the sentences. When the verb *wash*
indicates an action performed by an inanimate force then it seems less normal
to interpret *the pool* as a true undergoer which then may occur as the subject
of the sentence (giving it topic focus). Finally, when the undergoer fills the
grammatical function of subject or object, the scope (*pictures, glue* and *dirt*
in these examples) cannot be expressed in the same clause.[26] We can now
summarize the last section by giving the same information from another point
of view: that of using the interaction of surface structure functions (box 1)
and, the meanings of the fillers of these functions (box 4) to predict the
participant roles of the fillers. This approximates the point of view the
listener must take as he attempts to decode the speech signal. The verb *wash*
is inherently an action bitransitive verb. That is to say, it is an action and it

cooccurs with actor, undergoer and scope. If all three roles are realized and the sentence is active, then the subject must be the actor and the object is the scope (*glue*). If the sentence contains three roles and is passive, the subject is the scope, and the actor is expressed in a prepositional phrase introduced with *by*. If there are only two participants, then the subject may be either the scope or the undergoer. If the subject is the scope, then the other participant is the undergoer. (This is true whether the clause is active or passive.) If, on the other hand, the subject is the undergoer, then the other participant is the actor. (Again this is true, whether the clause is active or passive.)

One can see further effects of one box on another when one attempts to see the various types of concord relations. In these cases one usually finds information in one part of the description of one tagmeme affecting the choice of information given in a part of the description of another tagmeme. It is well known, for example, that *frighten* and *surprise* must take animate objects. We can say *He frightened the dog,* but not *He frightened the stone.*[27] The meaning of the verbs *frighten* and *surprise* require that their objects be animate. Thus we have information given in box 5 of the predicate requiring certain information in box 5 of the direct object.

	S	P Prn	He	P	VP	frightened		D.O.	NP	the dog
+				+			+			
	actor			P act				U	animate count concrete	

Compare this example with the fact that agreement between subjects and verbs in English is determined partly on the basis of the form of the subject and partly on the meaning. Subject nouns which have the form of plurals will cooccur with a plural form of the verb (*My pants are here*) while subject nouns which have the form of singulars will tend to cooccur with a singular form of the verb (*The book is here*) The problem comes when a noun may refer to groups of units. In this case, speakers referring to the group as a single coherent group will use singular concord (*The administration is against him,*) while speakers referring to the members of the group will use plural concord (*The administration are his friends*). In this example the form of the verb phrase is affected (box 2) and the controlling information is supplied by either the form of the subject noun phrase (box 2) or the meaning of the subject noun phrase (box 5).

The approach taken in the preceding discussion has assumed a normal or typical relation between the lexemic and the grammatical aspects of language.

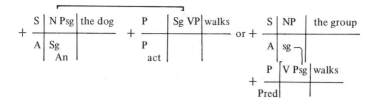

It implied for example, that the nucleus of a proposition was coextensive
with the nucleus of the grammatical clause which expressed that proposition,
and that the predicate of a proposition would be expressed by the predicate
of the clause which expressed that proposition. This is false. In fact the
theory must deal with a slippage between the lexemic and grammatical
aspects of language. Hale (1973b: 4-5),for example, suggests that sentences
such as *John is angry* be analyzed as subject + predicate + complement on the
level of surface grammar (to account for the fact that *be* inflects for tense,
number and person, and participates in modal and auxiliary constructions
similar to other predicates) but on the lexemic level he proposes that such
propositions contain within their lexemic predicate words like *angry* (to
account for the fact that it is the adjective which determines the role frame
for the proposition as a whole).

Similarly, the fact that adverbials of time and location are usually
optional, but are obligatory when certain verbs occur can be explained by
reference to the mismatch of the lexemic and grammatical aspects. If the
main verb of a clause is *put* for example, it must be followed by a location
modifier. Thus we can say *He put the butter on the table*, but not **He put
the butter*. This problem can be handled in the following way: Surface-
structure grammatical clauses may be transitive, and these transitive clauses
include in their margins optional tagmemes of location. Such tagmemes are
marginal and are regarded as less integrated in the action of the clause than
are the nuclear tagmemes of these constructions (subject, predicate, object).

Lexemic structures also have nuclei and margins. We can roughly define
the nucleus of a proposition, for example, as that portion of the proposition
which must be expressed in an independent clause. The proposition
underlying *He put the butter on the table* includes three participants within
its nucleus; the actor (*he*), the undergoer (*the butter*), and the scope (*on the
table*). One of these three participants, the scope, is realized as a marginal unit
in the surface structure, however.

We can now return to the examples involving *wash* and explain another
aspect of them. When we compare the meanings of I-i *John washed the glue
out of the shirts* with I-vii *John washed the shirts,* one of the differences we
find is that *the shirts* expresses a participant which seems to be more directly

involved in the action in vii than the same phrase does in i. This is difficult to account for if one only looks at the lexemic structure, but obvious if one looks at the surface grammar. In the one case that participant is expressed within the nucleus of the grammatical clause, while in the other, it is expressed via a (normally) optional clause level modifier occurring in the margin of the clause. A similar feature may be used to account for our initial reaction that *the glue* expressed an undergoer. In this case, *the glue* was expressed as a part of the nucleus of the grammatical clause. This implied that it was an integral part of the action, and there is a normal association of this role with the undergoer.

The next point in our discussion of the relation between the various types of information necessary for the description of the constructions of a language is to point out that there may be a mismatch between the lexemic and grammatical information. This has already been implied when it was stated (fn.21) that Hale analyzes clauses such as *John is tall* as consisting of two lexemic constituents: actor and predicate. This contrasts with his analysis of the surface structure of that clause into three constituents: subject, predicate and subject complement, Though grammatical predicates usually realize lexemic predicates, in this case the grammatical predicate does not realize any lexemic constituent and the grammatical subject complement realizes the lexemic predicate. While I suspect that many tagmemicists do not like this analysis, it is one which is allowed by the theory.

Another example with implications similar to the one above arises out of the discussion of modalities on propositions. (See section 3, above.) If we follow Halliday (1970) and say that sentence level modifiers such as *maybe* and *perhaps* are realizations of the same semantic system as are the modals in the verb phrase, then we have a single semantic system having relevance to the interpretation of the sentence as a whole, being realized at two points in the grammar, one a sentence level structure, but the other a phrase level structure. Again, we have a mismatch between the grammatical and lexemic aspects of language. This time, however, the mismatch is a mismatch involving the hierarchy.

Further evidence for the occasional mismatch between the lexemic and grammatical aspects of language comes from what I call displaced constituents. These are constituents which belong to one construction semantically, but have been moved to another construction to achieve some sort of focus or emphasis.[28] In the sentence *Only an occasional sailor walked by*, for example, the most normal interpretation of this sentence is not that the sailor sailed occasionally (thus making him an occasional sailor), but rather that individual sailors walked by occasionally. In other words, *occasional* is semantically a modifier of the verb *walked*, but grammatically a modiefier of the noun *sailor*. All the examples of this type that I have seen involve adverbs of frequency which are moved from a clause level modifier function to a prenominal modifier function. In the example above the clause level modifier is lowered and fills a role within the subject noun phrase. Other examples involve a kind of raising. In the sentence *This is the most frequent place that we've seen him*, the phrase *most frequent* grammatically modifies *place*, but lexemically modifies the verb in the relative clause which is contained within the noun phrase 'This is the place that we've seen him most frequently' .

The examples given here, though they are taken more or less at random should be sufficient to show that the lexemic and grammatical aspects of language, even though they usually correspond one to the other, may be varied independently of one another. As a result the two aspects must be specified independently. The new six-box notation for the description of tagmemes and syntagmemes is an attempt to do exactly that.

The revision of tagmemic theory and the six-box notation system intended to represent the new tagmeme and syntagmeme suggest a reinterpretation of some traditional problems. In particular, the concept of double function may be seen to be a special example of a general process of multiple structure for a given construction. Double function occurs when a constituent of a construction fills more than one grammatical function within that construction. In the question *Is John here?* , for example, the word *is* plays two grammatical roles. First, it is the main verb and tense marker of the clause. As such it fills the predicate function of the clause. In addition to this function, however, its occurrence before the subject indicates that this clause is a question. As a result we can say that *is* fills a second grammatical function, that of question marker.

The notion of double function just presented has been present in tagmemic theory ever since the early stages of the development of the theory.[29] In recent years, however, it has been seen that a much wider range of phenomena have multiple structure than had previously been believed. Within the grammatical aspect of language we may find that "...a structure may be a unit on one level, but be split into differing elements in relation to a higher level." (Pike - Pike, unpublished, chapter 2). Clauses of saying (*He said 'go'*) may be considered to be a single clause on one level, with *'go'* as the direct object of the verb *say*. But in the story in which this clause occurs the sequence *he said* will be considered "relevant to the level of reported monolog (margin as speech setting), with the quotation (no matter how long, whether of one or many sentences) as the nucleus of the reported monolog," (Pike - Pike, unpublished, chapter 2). These two examples imply that trees are not adequate to describe the surface grammatical structure of language within a tagmemic framework.

A third type of multiple structure involves multiple function in the lexemic aspect of language and often arises as a result of the use of nominalized clauses. As Pike and Pike say,

When a construction is modified in order to be used as a term in another construction, the new, derived construction picks up the roles normal to that new construction, but may also retain some of the roles of its source; the dual role may show up as the dual role of whatever tagmemes are retained during the derivation. (Pike - Pike, unpublished, Chapter 12).

Pike and Pike then discuss the structure of *his going saddened me*. In the structure of the including clause, *his going* fills the grammatical role of subject and the semantic role of actor. The internal structure of *his going* is complex, however. Pike and Pike call it a participial possessive nominal. The implications of this are that grammatically this construction may be analyzed as a margin (*his*) followed by a nucleus (*going*.) On the lexemic level, however, the analysis is more complex. On the one hand, *his going* is a nominalized clause. By means of the nominalization, the nucleus of the construction indicates an event and the margin a modifier of that event. But since the construction is a normalized clause it retains some of the characteristics of a clause. In particular, the lexemic relations of actor and action are preserved. Thus, *his* fills a margin function and has the two lexemic relations modifiers and actor, while *going* fills the nucleus function and has the two lexemic roles, event and action. Pike ans Pike represent this structure in the following way:

Part. Poss. Nom. Ph. = +	Mar	Poss Pro	+	Nuc	Pres Part
	Mod/A			Event/ Action	

This analysis raises some very interesting possibilities for analyzing certain ambiguities in the noun phrase. It is particularly relevant to the analysis of noun phrases which contain as their heads nouns which can be taken to refer to objects typically associated with certain activities. The noun *letter* is typically associated with the act of writing. As a result the phrase *George Washington's letter* is ambiguous in several ways. It may be a letter possessed by George Washington, a letter written by George Washington, or a letter written to George Washington. The first interpretation looks at a letter totally as an object. The other two interpretations regard the letter as the result of an act of writing. The act of writing may have an actor, an undergoer and a
     A   Sc U
scope (*John wrote Bill a letter.*) When *letter* is the head of a noun phrase,

either the actor or the scope may be realized as a possessive filling a margin function of the noun phrase. In the second interpretation George Washington is the actor while in the third interpretation George Washington is the scope. In other words, *George Washington's letter* may be interpreted as a nominalized clause.

I suspect that most tagmemicists would not like this analysis since it ranges pretty far from the actual surface structure. That is, in the example that the Pikes discuss there is good overt syntactic evidence for considering *his going* to be a nominalization of *he went*. In the case of *George Washington's letter* the only evidence I can see right now that this may be a nominalized clause is the lexemic interpretation of the possessive forms. There is a continuum between the two types of examples, however, so that any attempt to draw a line between those examples which are truely nominalized clauses and those which are not will be arbitrary. It can be shown that *his going* in *His going saddened me* is a weak nominalization by pointing out the fact that 1) clause level modifiers may maintain their adverbial form (*His quickly going saddened me*) and 2) the head may not be made plural (**His quickly goings saddened me.*). Between this weak nominalization and the true noun phrases are the strong nominalizations, such as gerunds. It can be shown that gerunds are derived from underlying clauses by performing such operations as substituting *ing* for the tense marker and all auxiliaries of the verb (e.g. *John's carvings of human heads.*) The fact that the head noun may be made plural indicates that it is a strong nominalization, as does the fact that adverbs which modify the underlying clause may not retain their adverbial form in the nominalization, (**John's quickly carvings of human heads.*) Strong nominalizations contain the same sorts of ambiguities as were discussed in the example of *George Washington's letter. John's carvings* may refer to the carvings that John possesses, those that John carved, or carvings that represent John. In the case of *John's carvings*, however, there is syntactic evidence to treat this phrase as a nominalized clause, while in the case of *George Washington's letter* only lexemic evidence exists which points toward treating that phrase as a nominalized clause.

SECTION V

As a final point it will be worthwhile to discuss recent developments in the formalisms used in tagmemic grammars. This topic has been of marginal interest to most tagmemicists, partly as a result of their background: Few tagmemicists have extensive training in working with formal systems. Another contributing factor to this lack of interest is an underlying belief that a completely adequate self-consistent formal system is impossible to achieve.

Indeed, for most tagmemicists, tagmemic rules are merely useful devices to express certain types of generalizations. If one wishes to make other generalizations than can be expressed within tagmemic formulae, then one reverts either to relatively ad-hoc representations within tagmemic formulae or to informal descriptions in English. In any case, the belief that no self-consistent formal system is completely adequate to describe all the aspects of language has precluded any major effort being spent on tagmemic formalism. Indeed the formalism has remained relatively constant until recent years.

From the beginning tagmemicists have used a formalism which makes their grammars look like context-free phrase-structure grammars. This formalism consists of a formula in which a syntagmeme is mentioned to the left of an equals-sign while the various tagmemes which together make up that syntagmeme are placed to the right of the equals-sign. e.g. Declarative Transitive Clause = + Subject: NP + Predicate: VP + Object: NP ± Time: Time Word ± Location: Location Word.

Each tagmeme consists of a label for a function (subject) and a label for the class of items which may fill that function (NP). In addition certain other features of each tagmeme are mentioned. The obligatory or optional occurrence of each tagmeme is represented by the + or ± placed in front of the function labels, and the order in which the tagmemes are mentioned within the formula represents the order in which they actually occur, (or, in languages with relatively free word order, a relatively frequent ordering.)

In spite of their similarity to phrase structure grammars I would claim that tagmemic grammars are not and have never been phrase-structure grammars in the sense defined by Chomsky (1963) and Postal (1964). In the first place, a syntagmeme is intended to be a contrastive construction type, and all the variants of that construction type are to be included within that formula. Thus even though the formula for a given syntagmeme must list the various tagmemes in one particular order, that syntagmeme is not restricted to one particular sequence of its constituents. All the following clauses, for example, belong to one syntagmeme in English.

John bought the store last year.
Last year John bought the store.
The store John bought last year.

Since phrase structure grammars in Chomsky's sense cannot reorder the constituents of a construction, such a phrase structure grammar could produce these clauses only by giving them different derivational histories.

Secondly, as was mentioned above (fn. 29), tagmemicists have long made use of the concept of double function. That is, it has long been possible within tagmemic theory for a given unit to fill two functions at the same time. It should be clear that no phrase structure grammar can produce such an analysis, but even more important, such an analysis cannot be represented by a simple tree structure.

While it can be shown that tagmemic grammars are not phrase-structure grammars, tagmemicists have been satisfied with a formalism which closely resembles that of phrase-structure grammars because they feel this formalism represents effectively the over-all patterns in the language. These patterns are of primary importance to tagmemicists. When restrictions on the cooccurrence of elements within a construction obscure these overall patterns, tagmemicists are reluctant to include a description of these restrictions within their formulas. This attitude is illustrated by the fact that Elson and Picket spend less than a page on how to describe restrictions on the cooccurrence of tagmemes within a syntagmeme. Most of the methods they suggest appear to be rather ad-hoc combinations of + and − and lines for connecting tagmemes which occur at some distance from one another. They suggest, for example, that two tagmemes which are not adjacent to each other and which are optional, but at least one of the two must occur, might be represented in the following way:

$$\pm \quad . \quad . \quad . \quad \pm$$
$$\underline{} + \underline{}$$

(Elson - Pickett 1962:60)

As tagmemicists, under the influence of transformational grammars, have felt the need to interpret their grammars as generative grammars, they have found it necessary to pay more attention to cooccurrence restrictions. They have not done this by changing their original notation system but by appending rules to each tagmemic formula which describe the various restrictions on that formula. Hollenbach illustrates this approach with a discussion of Spanish noun phrases:

If a syntagmeme is defined as a structure which can be described truthfully by a single formula, then one type of Spanish noun phrases groups into four different syntagmemes: masculine singular noun phrase, masculine plural noun phrase, feminine singular noun phrase, and feminine plural noun phrase. This analysis is obviously counter-intuitive; el alumno bueno 'the good (male) pupil', and las alumnas buenas 'the good (female) pupils' both manifest a determiner-head-modifier structure. The solution advocated in the present paper is to posit one structure, described by a single formula which generates correct strings, illustrated above, but also such incorrect ones as *las alumno buenos. A rule following the formula states that the noun phrase is the domain of the categories gender and number, and that article and adjective word structures manifesting the determiner and modifier tagmemes are restricted to those which agree in gender and number with the noun word structure manifesting the head tagmeme. This rule eliminates sixty of sixty-four possible combinations of the two categories in this phrase. (Hollenbach 1968:55)

Jacobs and Longacre (1967) present a more formal (and less readable) version of this approach. While this method of indicating restrictions is not elegant in that it is added on to the formulas in an ad-hoc way, it has the advantage of not obscuring the essential insights which are gained by looking at the overall pattern while allowing the grammarian to describe only the forms which actually occur. The concept of rules which apply to syntagmemes has been extended recently by Pike and Pike (1974) to apply to tagmemes. Thus, in that recent discussion of the English verb phrase, they index a number of tagmemes with a marker which refers to a particular rule which applies to those tagmemes. The purpose of these rules is to describe the effect each tagmeme has on the immediately following tagmemes. Thus the tagmeme which is filled by the modal verbs is indexed by a marker which refers to a rule which suppresses the inflection of the following verb stem. This of course accounts for the existence of sequences such as

he may have come
he may be coming
he may come

and the absence of sequences such as

*he may has come
*he may been eating
*he may coming

It is important to notice that these indices are not merely appended to the formula as a whole as were the rules Longacre worked with, they are now an integral part of the tagmemes which introduce them. They are not considered separate units in their own right.

> The rules are emic features of the tagmemes, rather than themselves being emic units in their own right (Pike - Pike 1974: 176).

Pike and Pike point out the similarity between what they are proposing now and features of tagmemes which had been mentioned earlier. Placement rules, for example, whereby a tagmeme was given more than one possible location within the syntagmeme, have been in existence since the beginning of tagmemics. Similarly, it has always been necessary to indicate whether a tagmeme was obligatory or optional. The primary difference between what is proposed now and what has been used before is that now we are looking at the effect of the tagmeme on other tagmemes, rather than at features that concern solely that tagmeme.

The Pikes point out that tagmemic descriptions require two different types of rules: 1) monolevel rules and 2) multilevel rules. Monolevel rules affect elements of the string as wholes. Thus a rule describing the possibility in English of placing the direct object first in its clause (*That I know* vs. *I know that*) would be a monolevel rule since it affects the total string which fills the object tagmeme as a unit. Multilevel rules, on the other hand, affect various portions of a filler of a tagmeme. A good example of this is the rule mentioned above in which the filler of the tagmeme which follows the modal will not contain an inflectional affix. In this case, a phrase-level index affects the internal structure of the word which fills the following phrase level tagmeme. We therefore have an index which has its source at the phrase-level affecting the structure of a word-level construction.

It is important to stress that multilevel rules are not being discovered now, for tagmemicists have always had to deal with subclasses of constructions which are determined on the basis of distribution. In a grammar of English one needed to distinguish, for example, at least four different types of prepositional phrases depending on whether they filled time, instrument, location, or accompaniment functions in the clause. This was determined in part by figuring out whether the noun phrase which was the object of the preposition denoted a time instrument, place or accompaniment. This could only be determined by looking at the noun which filled the function of head of the noun phrase, to see if it denoted a time (*at that time*), an instrument (*with a knife*), or a place (*at the house*),or something similar to the subject of the clause (*John came with the boys*). Note that in these examples the clause structure affects the structure of word-level constructions. This sort of example has always been dealt with in that the filler class of a tagmeme has always been considered a distinctive feature of the tagmeme. What is new here is that a) it is now seen that the presence of one tagmeme may affect the structure of the filler of another, and b) this effect may be considered a distinctive feature of that tagmeme. As a final point on the formalism used in tagmemic grammars, we must mention the attempt to represent the correlation of the grammatical, leximic, and phonological aspects of language. Syntagmemes are no longer composed of tagmemes which are simply correlations of a grammatical function with the class of grammatical units which may fill that function. Instead each tagmeme is a correlation of each of the three aspects of language. In addition, each of the aspects of language has a function which is correlated with a class of units which can fill that function. This results in the nine-box tagmeme mentioned on page.... While this notation system is not entirely satisfactory[30] it has already proven to be of great use heuristically in making tagmemic grammars.

SECTION VI

In conclusion I would like to re-emphasize the major tenets underlying tagmemic theory as it applies to grammatical analysis[31]. Language is a part of behavior and cannot be divorced from its behavioral matrix. This leads to the division between form and function. No function exists without some form to fill it, and no form is of interest unless it fills some function. Thus form and function, though independent, are related. The items which fill each function are units. The units may be simple morphemes, or they may be complex, in which case they are syntagmemes (or patterns).

In addition to playing a function within a larger unit each syntagmeme in a language is a part of a system of contrasting syntagmemes. The total system of contrasting syntagmemes of a given type (e.g. clause) is called a level. The total number of contrastive levels in a language is a hierarchy. Each language has three hierarchies, a phonological hierarchy, a grammatical hierarchy and a lexemic hierarchy. Each of these is independent of the others though related to each of the others.

NOTES

1 Recently Longacre and a number of other tagmemicists have relaxed this requirement and now deal with deep structures which do not have a simple relation to the stream of speech (for examples, see Ballard-Conrad-Longacre 1971a, 1971b, Longacre 1972). Pike still holds pretty strictly to the requirement that all units have both a form and a meaning. This is not to say that he *never* breaks this rule, but rather that he does so only when he sees no possible way to preserve the direct correlation of form and function.
2 It is true that one can easily find surface structure differences such as the differences between interrogative and declarative clauses which correlate directly with differences in the underlying structures. Other surface-structure differences, however, such as the difference between *John saw the dog* and *The dog was seen by John*, do not correlate with differences in the deep structure. Similarly, one cannot define the subject of a clause as that clause-level constituent which indicates the actor of the predication. Instead the subject of a clause has a particular relation to the clause as a whole. In English it seems to be the topic of the clause. It has the formal features of being that clause-level constituent which in a positive declarative clause precedes the tense marker of the verb, and, if the verb is in the present tense, agrees in number with the verb. It is true that subjects are very often the actors of the predications of which they form a part. This is frequently not the case, however. Hence, it is impossible to use the correlation of subject and performer as a means of defining the notion of subject. It would seem, then, that it is rarely necessary to refer to underlying structure when discussing surface structure relations, and it is rarely necessary to refer to specific surface structure relations when discussing underlying structures (beyond the proviso that these underlying structures have at least *some* surface realization).
3 Longacre (1965) uses the term *matrix* instead of *field*. I prefer *field* or *system* for two reasons. First of all, *matrix* refers to a visual n-dimensional array which may be used to

represent a system of a language (each dimension of the array representing a parameter of the system). Since I believe the things said here have some relevance for a language system, not merely its visual representation, I prefer to use *system* and *field* which directly refer to the objects being described. My second objection to the use of the term *matrix* is that on a number of occasions within tagmemic literature, matrices have been used to represent objects other than systems. Pike (1970: 38) presents a 'Co-Occurrence Matrix of Bimoba Clauses in Clusters'. This matrix is no more than a chart of the various clause types which may co-occur within a clause cluster. No attempt is made to state that this chart represents a system of the language. The term *System* has not, to my knowledge, been applied to such a representation. I prefer to use the terms which exclude such charts, hence I will restrict myself to the term *system*.

4 What follows in this section is a summary with some revision of my "Some fundamental insights of tagmemics revisited".

5 See Bolinger (1967) for a detailed discussion with many examples.

6 While this example does not pretend to describe any actual language, examples similar to the one presented here may be found in Trique (Longacre 1966:244) Lamani (Trail 1970:38, 50-51) and Totonac (Reid - Bishop - Button - Longacre 1968:31, 34, 44)

7 The Pikes use terms such as *proposition* to refer to a much less abstract concept than do the transformational grammarians. A number of transformational grammarians analyze the phrase *the child in the water* as containing three propositions in its underlying structure. First, that an individual is in something, second, something is water, and third, the individual is a child. The Pikes would deny propositional status to these since they are not realized as either clauses or sentences. It should be noted that the discussion in this section refers to the normal situation. Exceptions to the norm occur for a number of specific reasons. If a nominalized clause is used, for example, as a term in a proposition (e.g. *John's coming early surprised Mary*) then that construction (*John's coming early*, in the example above) will have both the meaning of a proposition and the meaning of a term.

8 Differences in the specific interpretations of one lexemic role in different sentences can be accounted for by differences in the lexemic features of the participants which fill that role in the two sentences. Thus, the difference in the interpretation of the lexemic role of actor in 1) and 2) below will be accounted for by reference to the difference in the lexemic features of *the men* and *the locomotive*; specifically, *the men* denotes an animate participant while *the locomotive* an inanimate participant. 1) *The men cleared the tracks*. 2) *The locomotive cleared the tracks*.

9 By using the term *referent* I do not intend to imply that tagmemicists are interested in nouns to the exclusion of other parts of speech. This term should rather be interpreted to mean the particular real world item, act, situation, quality, etc. to which a particular construction refers in a particular place in a text. Thus the referent of a clause would be the particular state or act to which it refers when it is used.

10 It should be emphasized in view of the limited number of roles they use, that Pike and Pike are attempting here only to account for the lexemic relations they find realized within the nucleus of a clause. Presumably, when they attempt to expand their view to include the various clause-level margins (in particular, the various types of adverbial modifiers of clauses), their inventory of semantic relations will have to be expanded. One wonders however, whether after they have accounted for the marginal portions of clauses they will still be able to preserve both the generality of the relationships they treat and the Fillmorean restriction that any given role may occur only once within a single clause. At present, since they treat only the nucleus of the clause, this restriction still holds.

11 For an extensive list of the modifiers similar in function to *maybe*, see the discussion of attitudinal truth-value disjuncts in Quirk *et al* (1972, section 8.82 ff.) The other attitudinal disjuncts they discuss (e.g. *fortunately, understandably, wisely,* etc.) may also belong here, though this is less certain.

44

12 Verbs such as *think* and *believe* are primarily verbs which take a (deformed) sentence in their object. In this primary use one can say that a sentence such as *I think that he came* is an assertion about what John thinks (cf. *I believe this is an example of Byzantine art*). Because of their meaning, however (as opposed to the meaning of *know*) they have taken on the function of toning down the assertional value of the clause which occurs as their object. In extreme cases this down-toning function seems to be the only function these words have in the sentence, and their meanings are very similar to those of *maybe* and *perhaps*. The following example from Thurber illustrates this use. "Here lies Miss Groby, not dead, I think, but put away on a shelf with the other T squares and rulers whose edges had lost their certainty." (*The Thurber Carnival*, p. 52). In this example one could substitute *maybe* or *perhaps* for *I think* with minimal disruption of either the grammar or the semantics of this sentence.

13 Another type of construction whose meaning does not seem to be accounted for within the levels of deep structure we have mentioned so far is the sentence modifier which relates to the act of speaking rather than to the content of the sentence of which it is a part. I refer here to style disjuncts (see Quirk *et al* 1972 section 8.80 for a discussion and list) such as *frankly, briefly, approximately, confidentially*, etc. (e.g. *Frankly, I am tired.*), and to clauses expressing cause, reason, condition, etc. for speaking (e.g. *Does he have a flashlight? Because if he doesn't we'd better bring ours.* and *There's a post office in Weidman if you want to go there.*). These examples are not examples of new meanings, however. It is already necessary to describe relations such as cause and condition to account for relations between clauses. Similarly, one must, within a proposition, account for the meanings of adverbs of manner (e.g. *to speak frankly*). As a result, these examples are unaccounted for only because the modifiers and subordinate clauses refer directly to the act of communication which is taking place at the time of speaking (writing). If we say that anything which relates directly to the interaction of the participants in a communicative act belongs to the calculus of repartee, then we have here a kind of semantic level skipping.

14 All verbs which occur in the description of the meaning of the phrase but which do not occur in the phrase itself are added purely for stylistic reasons. In a more formal phrasing the meaning would be expressed as follows:

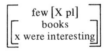

15 A few modifiers seem to have this relation to the referent of the noun phrase. The first noun phrase of *three different people told Bill* (where *different* emphasises the unconnectedness of the people rather than how they compare with the rest of society) cannot be interpreted as three x_{pl} such that x are people and x are different. We must rather say that we have three different (unconnected) x_{pl} (X_1 X_2 X_3) such that x are people. Examples of similar modifiers are *various* (*their various colors*), *certain* (*certain unidentified sources*), *specific* (*your specific new plant needs*) and *other* (*your other raincoats*).

16 Two other modifiers which seem to be referent modifiers are active infinitive phrases ([*He had*] *no children to succeed him.*) and retroactive infinitive phrases ([*He brought*] *a story for us to read.* [*All I need is*] *a bed to sleep in*]. I have not yet been able to devise a satisfying method for representing the difference in meaning between these modifiers, and relative clauses.

17 This is not to be interpreted that we analyze intensifiers and modalities in the same way, but rather we note that they seem to do similar things to the constructions they modify.

18 A number of other types of modifiers remain to be accounted for. I refer in particular to the noun phrase complements (*the news that he had come, our duty to*

preserve our heritage, an error of .01 degree). These differ from all the other modifiers that we have discussed in that these identify the referent of the noun phrase rather than give more attributes. Thus, in the first example, the news was that he had come. This sense of double identification of the referent is so strong that a number of traditional grammarians have treated these constructions as appositive constructions, (similar to *John, who was beside me, was not injured by the blast.).*

19 The nouns which may be used in this function are not restricted to common nouns but also include proper names. To say *That man is a veritable Socrates* is to say that he possesses attributes (wisdom) for which Socrates was famous. It is also worth emphasizing that only some of the attributes are important in this type of construction. Socrates presumably had many attributes, some good and some bad. He is known in our culture primarily for being wise. Hence to say *Bill is a veritable Socrates* is a way of saying Bill is wise; it is not a way of saying Bill has a bad temper or Bill talks a great deal. Similarly when we say *Bill is a diplomat* we are referring to a limited set of attributes which our culture believes diplomats ought to have. Thus *Bill is a diplomat* will mean that Bill is good at reconciling differences but it will not mean that Bill lies a great deal.

20 It is interesting to note that the so-called independent relative clauses (*Bill took whatever he wanted*) can be interpreted in a way that exactly parallels the interpretation of normal relative clauses, within a noun phrase except that the independent relative clause is the only source of information about the referent. Thus the interpretation of the example above would be roughly, 'Bill took any x such that he wanted x'. Independant relative clauses have co-occurrence restrictions similar to the co-occurrence restrictions on noun phrases. Thus parallel to *The ghost frightened John* we find *The ghost frightened whoever and whatever it could*, in which we know that *whoever* and *whatever* refer to animate beings. Similarly, we accept *What he put on her foot was warm and sticky.* but not **what he put on her foot was beauty.* since *warm* and *sticky* are attributes which may be applied to concrete objects, the sorts of things one can put on someone's foot. On the other hand, one cannot handle abstract ideas; as a result we do not accept the second sentence. In summary, then, we can interpret independent relative clauses as special kinds of noun phrases which happen to consist solely of a relative clause.

21 The Pikes do not consider complement in their classification of predication types. I suspect they do not because complement occupies an ambiguous role within their system. Hale (1973b:5) even suggests that the adjective phrases in *John was angry at me* and *John was tall* be analyzed as predicates rather than as complements in the underlying structure. Hale's analysis has strongly influenced the Pikes' work (witness the fact that the chart below is called the Hale chart), and I suspect that even though they have rejected his particular analysis of complement they have retained his feeling that complements are not independent of predicates. In fact, if complements are to be separated from predicates, then they make good candidates for subcategorizing clause types since complement seems to be required in the two semireceptive clause types and the state-eventive-clause type. In addition, complement may be added to almost all of the other clause types. e.g. *She left the room* vs. *She left the room messy.* One could indeed say that *She left the room messy* involves a nesting of predications, roughly 'she left (the room was messy)'. But this argument also applies to most of the examples of scope (when it is neither subject nor object). Thus *We keep the money in a box* could be analyzed as 'we keep (the money is in a box)'; I would therefore suggest that the taxonomy presented by the Pikes could be improved by treating complement and scope in parallel ways.

22 When I say forms here, I am focussing on: 1) the surface grammatical functions (Subj., Pred., obj., etc., including the presence or absence of passive in the verb phrase.) 2) the various participant roles which may fill these functions, 3) which of these functions are obligatory, which are optional and which are obligatorily absent, and under what conditions.

23   Example III-viii is not grammatical, hence we cannot interpret *down stream* as undergoer.

24   I can find no English example provided by the Pikes or Hale in which scope occurs without some other participant role (at least complement).

25   An implication of this analysis is that *off the wall, the shirts,* and *the pool* must indicate the undergoer. We are forced to this conclusion because a) each participant role may only occur once within a clause and b) There are only four participant roles available in this model, two of which, actor and undergoer, have already been used in this clause. That leaves complement and scope as the possible roles. These clearly do not fill the role of complement. While I do not find this analysis satisfying, I find that Pike and Pike have analyzed a sentence similar to the ones we have worked with, *She wrung water out of the clothes,* as containing *water* as an object-as-scope. I believe this implies that *out of the clothes* (since this is obligatory in this sentence) must indicate the undergoer. Since I am referring to a preliminary version of their material this may be an analysis which they will wish to change.

26   The fact that at least one of the restrictions in the last paragraph is based on the semantic interpretation of the verb *wash* bodes ill for an attempt made by Hale to set up paradigms of clause derivations. Hale says:

> The notion, clause pattern, includes not only that basic, simple, relatively underived clause which most easilly and clearly fits into a given cell in the Hale chart, but also the total set of clauses that derive from it. (Hale 1973b: 14).

Or again:

> A contrastive clause type is viewed as a paradigm of clauses linked by derivational rules. One member of this paradigm is taken to be the basic member of the type. The other members are viewed as derived variants of the type. A given paradigm will have numerous examples. Within a given example of a paradigm, all variants will share the same verb... A contrastive clause type is thus exemplified as a set of variant clauses which are related to one another by rule and which share the same verb. (Hale and Watters 1973: 179-80)

It should be clear from the passages quoted that if this classification into paradigms is to be useful, it must apply to all clauses which have a particular form. The examples given in I, II, and III above, however, show that the particular variations in the meaning of the predicate and the meanings of the other participants in the proposition have a strong influence on the derivations which are available to a particular sentence. It remains only to say that this interaction of word meanings and paradigms is very frequent. As a result, it seems to me that the only way such an approach could work would be to set up emic paradigms containing certain crucial clause forms essential to the paradigms together with marginal clause forms which a given contrastive clause type may or may not enter into.

27   It is worth noting here that the categorization of objects into animate and inanimate objects is, like all categorizations, an arbitrary one imposed on reality. As a result we find the border between the two categories fuzzy and liable to shift depending on one's point of view toward the object being categorized. Thus, one can set up a continuum of examples ranging from fully acceptable to unacceptable depending on whether a person is willing to assign animateness to a particular thing.

> *He frightened the dog.*
> *He frightened the caterpillar.*
> *He frightened the tree.*
> *He frightened the paremecium/virus.*
> *He frightened the stone.*

In cultures which believe that all things live and have spirits, all these sentences (or their translations) would be acceptable. For me, however, the caterpillar example is marginal, and all the ones after are unacceptable.

28 Since focus usually results from discourse level considerations, a discussion of the factors affecting the use of these constructions will probably involve considerations outside the clause and sentences in which they occur.

29 Hart (1957), for example, uses the concept of double function in her description of emphatic clauses and query clauses.

30 I suspect, for example, that it will be difficult to use this notation system to describe displaced constituents (see sec. 4, above) in a principled way.

31 One major tenet, that no single point of view is sufficient to adequately account for all aspects of language, has not been discussed in this paper due to exigencies of time and space. Since this has not been discussed, it has not been included in the summary even though it is an important distinctive feature of tagmemics. See the last chapter of this volume, by K.L. Pike, for a discussion of this point.

REFERENCES

Ballard, D. Lee, Robert J. Conrad - Robert Longacre
  1971a "The deep and surface grammar of interclausal relations", *Foundations of Language* 7: 70-118.
  1971b *More on the deep and surface grammar of interclausal relations, Language Data, Asian-Pacific Series*, 1, (Santa Ana [now Huntington Beach, Calif.]: Summer Institute of Linguistics.)
Becker, Alton L.
  1967a "Conjoining in a tagmemic grammar of English," *Monograph Series on Language and Linguistics* 20 (Washington, D.C.: Georgetown University Press), 109-22.
  1967b *A generative description of the English subject tagmeme*, Phd. Dissertation, University of Michigan.
Bolinger, Dwight L.
  1967 "Adjectives in English: Attribution and predication." *Lingua* 18: 1-34.
Brend, Ruth M. (Ed.)
  1974 *Advances in tagmemics*. (Amsterdam: North-Holland Publishing Co.)
Chomsky, Noam
  1963 "Formal properties of grammars", *Handbook of Mathematical Psychology*, 2, Ed. by Luce, Bush and Galanter (Somerset, New Jersey: John Wiley and Sons), 323-418.
Cook, Walter A.
  1971 "Case grammar as a deep structure in tagmemic analysis", *Languages and Linguistics: Working Papers* 2, (Washington, D.C.: Georgetown Univ. Press), 1-9.
  1972 "A set of postulates for case grammar analysis", *Languages and Linguistics: Working Papers* 4 (Washington, D.C.; Georgetown Univ. Press), 35-49.
Elson, Benjamin - Velma Pickett
  1962 *An introduction to morphology and syntax* (Santa Ana [now Huntington Beach, Calif.]: Summer Institute of Linguistics.).
Fillmore, Charles C.
  1966 "A proposal concerning English prepositions", *Monograph Series on Languages and Linguistics* [Ohio State University] 19: 19-33.
  1968 "The case for case", *Universals in linguistic theory*, ed. by E. Bach and R. Harms (New York: Holt, Rinehart and Winston), 1-88.

Fries, Peter H.
  1970 *Tagmeme sequences in the English noun phrase* (Santa Ana: Summer Institute of Linguistics Publications in Linguistics and Related Fields, 36).
  1974 "Some fundamental insights of tagmemics revisited", in Brend 1974: 23-34
Hale, Austin
  1973a [Ed.] *Clause, sentence and discourse patterns in selected languages of Nepal,* Parts I-IV (Santa Ana: Summer Institute of Linguistics Publications in Linguistics and Related Fields 40).
  1973b "Toward the systematization of display grammar", in Hale 1973a, Part I, 1-37.
Hale, Austin - David Watters
  1973 "A survey of clause patterns", in Hale 1973a, Part II: 175-249.
Halliday, M.A.K.
  1970 "Functional diversity in language as seen from a consideration of modality and mood in English", *Foundations of Language* 6: 322-61.
Hart, Helen Long
  1957 "Hierarchical structuring of Amuzgo grammar", *International Journal of American Linguistics* 23: 141-64.
Hollenbach, Barbara Erickson
  1968 "Construction types as linguistic units", *Linguistics* 39: 50-58.
Jacobs, Kenneth - Robert E. Longacre
  1967 "Patterns and rules in Tzotzil grammar", *Foundations of Language* 3: 325-89.
Lakoff, George
  1970 *Irregularity in syntax* (New York: Holt, Rinehart and Winston).
Liem, Nguyen Dang
  1966 *English grammar: A combined tagmemic and transformational approach,* Linguistic Circle of Canberra Publications, Series C, Vol. 1.
Longacre, Robert E.
  1964 *Grammar discovery procedures* (The Hague: Mouton and Co.) (=*Janua Linguarum, series minor* 33).
  1965 "Some fundamental insights of tagmemics", *Language* 41: 65-76.
  1966 "Trique clause and sentence: a study in contrast, variation and distribution", *International Journal of American Linguistics* 32: 242-52.
  1970 "Sentence structure as a statement calculus", *Language* 46, 783-815.
  1972 *Hierarchy and universality of discourse constituents in New Guinea languages: discussion* (Washington, D.C.: Georgetown University Press).
Pike, Kenneth L.
  1964 "Discourse analysis and tagmeme matrices", *Oceanic Linguistics* 3: 5-25
  1967 *Language in relation to a unified theory of the structure of human behavior* (2nd revised edition) (The Hague: Mouton and Co.)
  1970 *Tagmemic and matrix linguistics applied to selected African languages* (Santa Ana: Summer Institute of Linguistics Publications in Linguistics and Related Fields: 23).
Pike, Kenneth L. - Evelyn G. Pike
  1973 Grammatical Analysis [mimeo]
  1974 "Rules as components of tagmemes in the English verb phrase", in Brend 1974: 175-204
Platt, John T.
  1971 *Grammatical form and grammatical meaning* (Amsterdam: North-Holland Publishing Co.)
Postal, Paul
  1964 *Constituent structure: a study of contemporary models of syntactic description,* Bloomington, Ind.: Indiana University Research Center Publications in Anthropology, Folklore, and Linquistics 30.

Quirk, Randolph - Sidney Greenbaum - Geoffrey Leech - Jan Svartvik
    1972 *Grammar of contemporary English* (New York: Seminar Press).
Reid, Aileen - Ruth G. Bishop – Ella M. Button - Robert E. Longacre
    1968 *Totonac: From clause to discourse* (Santa Ana: Summer Institute of
    Linguistics Publications in Linguistics and Related Fields 17).
Trail, Ronald
    1970 *The grammar of Lamani* (Santa Ana: Summer Insittute of Linguistics
    Publications in Linguistics and Related Fields 24).
    1973 "Semantic relations between whole propositions in English", *Patterns in
    clause, sentence, and discourse in selected languages of Nepal* (Santa Ana:
    Summer Institute of Linguistics Publications in Linguistics and Related
    Fields 41, Part I), 5-34
Weinreich, Uriel
    1966 "Explorations in semantic theory", *Current Trends in Linguistics* 3:
    Theoretical foundations, ed. by T.A. Sebeok (The Hague: Mouton and Co.),
    395-477.
Wise, Mary Ruth
    1971 *Identification of participants in discourse* (Santa Ana: Summer Institute of
    Linguistics Publications in Linguistics and Related Fields 28).

THE RELATIONSHIP OF TAGMEMIC THEORY TO RULES, DERIVATION, AND TRANSFORMATIONAL GRAMMAR

AUSTIN HALE

Summer Institute of Linguistics, Nepal

Tagmemics was born as the result of a search for units of grammar which would have the same kind of usefulness as phonemes have in phonology or as morphemes have in lexicon.[1] Tagmemics is and remains heavily unit-oriented. The goals of tagmemics are goals of communicative acculturation. In developing tagmemics, Pike has attempted to provide the nonnative participant in a given culture with the best possible tools for mastering the communicative systems of the culture, both verbal and nonverbal. From this point of view, mastering a communicative system involves learning to use and understand the units, the patterned 'chunks' of communicative behavior which comprise the heart of the system. It involves learning what systematic physical differences serve to distinguish and identify various units in various systems. It involves learning the various physical representations that a given unit can have and still remain the same unit for communicative purposes. It involves learning where such a unit can be used appropriately — where it belongs in terms of class, sequence, and system. In most tagmemic descriptions underlying structures consist exclusively of units. The units of which underlying structures consist are arranged in three simultaneous hierarchies. They can be viewed by an observer from three different perspectives. They have functions relevant to a larger social context. Within tagmemics, units are taken much more seriously than rules.

It would be misrepresenting the case to insist that tagmemics claims only to be a tool. Any view as helpful as tagmemics is in communicative acculturation must incorporate something deeply true (as the participant observer can perceive truth) about communicative human nature. Tagmemics claims to have grasped certain fundamental defining characteristics of human nature and has made use of them in a general heuristic of human communicative behavior.[2]

Transformational Grammar, on the other hand, was born as the result of a search for a formal characterization of human linguistic competence. It represents a serious attempt to determine the formal and explicit set of rules that can serve as a generative definition of the set of sentences which belong to a particular language. It also represents an attempt to define the form of grammar which can serve as an explicit definition of human language in general. With the recursive properties of language in heavy focus, the notion of unit was subordinated to the notion of rule. Category symbols such as NP and VP are chosen because the rules need such symbols if they are to operate correctly. While the transformational NP's and VP's may in some sense be thought of as analogous to the units of tagmemics, they are certainly not presented as specific contrastive structures occurring at specific emic levels of the grammatical hierarchy.[3]

It would be as difficult to write a coherent essay defining the units of transformational grammar as it is to write an account of the formal definition of rules in tagmemics. The various active proponents of tagmemics appear to share far more of what they believe about units than they share regarding the use of rules in a tagmemic description. In any event one must make some sense of the notion of underlying structure in tagmemics if one is to make sense of the rules which apply to underlying structure. For this reason we haven chosen to divide our discussion into two sections: 1) Underlying structure in tagmemics, and 2) Rules in tagmemics. The relationship of tagmemics to transformational grammar will be dealt with in both of these sections.

1. UNDERLYING STRUCTURE IN TAGMEMICS.

The term *underlying structure* as used here is not at all equivalent to the notion of deep structure. Rather, it will be used to refer to those abstract representations within a description to which the rules apply in the generation of particular examples in a given language. It also refers to the apparatus which summarizes the possible range of variation of a particular unit without actually specifying the narrow phonological, lexical, and grammatical form of a specific utterance.

This section represents an attempt to determine the constraints that tagmemics places upon underlying structure. If we take the function of rules in a tagmemic grammar to be that of mapping underlying structure onto the most shallow representation given to an utterance in each of the three hierarchies, then limitations upon underlying structures are also limitations upon rules. Discussions of limitations upon underlying structure representations are far more accessible within the literature on tagmemics than are discussions of rules. It is for this reason that this rather indirect approach to the topic has been chosen.

1.1. *An early transformational view of the English auxiliary.* One way of seeing certain constraints that tagmemics imposes upon underlying structures is to look at tagmemic objections to certain underlying structures which have been proposed within transformational studies of English. In *Syntactic structures* Chomsky used an interesting analysis of the English auxiliary to demonstrate how a complex bit of English could be rather simply described if transformational rules were incorporated into the description. Within this approach, rules have descriptive priority over units. Elements such as NP and VP are justified to a large extent in terms of the rules that refer to them. The relevant phrase structure rules are as follows (Chomsky 1957: 39, 111-113).

1.	Sentence	$\dashrightarrow$	NP + VP
2.	VP	$\dashrightarrow$	Verb + NP
3.	NP	$\dashrightarrow$	$\left\{ \begin{array}{l} NP_{sing} \\ NP_{pl} \end{array} \right\}$
...			
8.	Verb	$\dashrightarrow$	Aux + V
9.	V	$\dashrightarrow$	*hit, take, walk, read,* etc.
10.	Aux	$\dashrightarrow$	C (M) (*have* +en) (*be* +ing) (*be* + en)
11.	M	$\dashrightarrow$	*will, can, may, shall, must*

These rules produce underlying structures such as Tree 1.

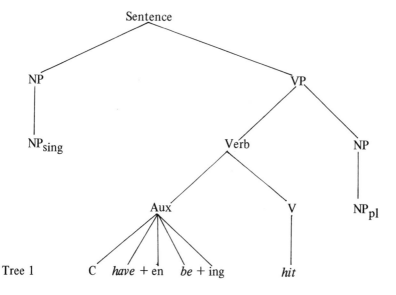

Tree 1

54

To the underlying structure represented by Tree 1 the Number Transformation obligatorily applies

15. Number Transformation – obligatory
     Structural analysis: X – C – Y
     Structural change: C - - - → $\left\{\begin{array}{l} \text{S in the context NP}_{\text{sing}} \\ \phi \text{ in other contexts} \\ \text{past in any context} \end{array}\right\}$

When Rule 15 applies to Tree 1 it substitutes an S for the C which is the leftmost constituent of Aux.[4] The output of Rule 15 is also an underlying structure. Rule 20, Auxiliary Transformation, obligatory applies to the output of Rule 15.

20. Auxiliary Transformation -- obligatory
     Structural analysis: X – Af – V – Y
     (where Af is any C or is *en* or *ing*;
        V is any M or V, or *have* or *be*)
     Structural change: $X_1 - X_2 - X_3 - X_4$
        $\cdots \rightarrow X_1 - X_3 - X_2 - X_4$

When Rule 20 applies to the output of Rule 15 the result is an underlying structure which includes a subtree something like[5] Tree 2

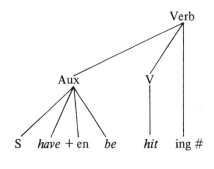

Tree 2

Having applied once, Rule 20 must now apply again to its own output, producing a structure something like Tree 3.

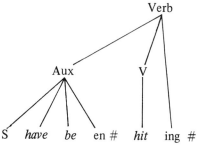

Tree 3

Since Rule 20 is obligatory and since Tree 3 still has a sequence which can be analyzed as X – Af – v – Y, Rule 20 must apply once more, yielding a structure something like Tree 4.

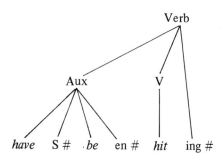

Tree 4

The word boundaries which occur between each Af and its following v now prevent Rule 20 from applying again to Tree 4. Rule 21, Word Boundary Transformation is now called upon to insert additional word boundaries between each pair of elements in the terminal string which is not of the form, v followed by Af.

21.   Word Boundary Transformation -- obligatory
      Structural analysis: X – Y (where X ≠ v or Y ≠ Af)
      Structural change: $X_1 - X_2 \cdots \rightarrow X_1 - \# X_2$

When Rule 21 applies to Tree 4, Tree 5 results:

56

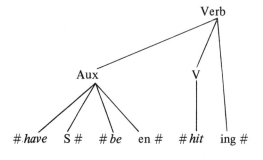

Tree 5

Certain other rules relevant to the derivation of the auxiliary may apply in other instances. There is, for example, an optional negative transformation which may apply to a structure like Tree 1.

16. T_{not} – optional
     Structural analysis:
     $$\left\{ \begin{array}{l} NP - C - V \ldots \\ NP - C + M - \ldots \\ NP - C + \text{have} - \ldots \\ NP - C + \text{be} - \ldots \end{array} \right\}$$

     Structural change: $X_1 - X_2 - X_3 \cdots \rightarrow X_1 - X_2 + \text{n't} - X_3$

There is also an optional contrastive stress transformation which may apply to a structure like Tree 1.

17. T_A -- optional
     Structural analysis: same as 16
     Structural change: $X_1 - X_2 - X_3 \cdot \rightarrow X_1 - X_2 + A - X_3$

When morphophonemic rules apply to Tree 5 we get

   ...has been hitting ...

If Rule 16 had applied between Tree 1 and Tree 2 we would have gotten

   ...hasn't been hitting ....

If Rule 17 had applied but not Rule 16, we would have gotten

   ...has been hitting ...

If Rules 16 and 17 had both applied, the result would have been

... hasn't been hitting ...

The consequences of Rules 16 and 17 are somewhat different if the original underlying structure is Tree 6

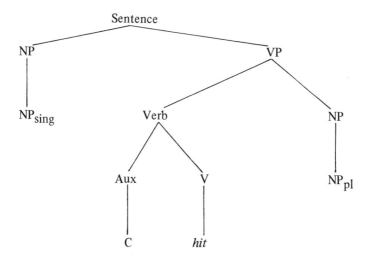

Tree 6

In this case Rule 15, Number Transformation, will apply as usual. If Rule 16, T_{not}, is allowed to apply at this point, Tree 7 will result.

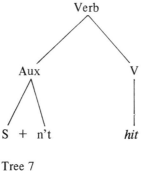

Tree 7

The presence of the negative *n't* between S and *hit* then takes this structure

58

out of the range of the auxiliary transformation. Rule 20 does not apply. Instead, there is another rule (one of two that are numbered 21) which is called *do*-Transformation and which applies after the insertion of word boundaries.

21'   *do*-Transformation -- obligatory:
        Structural analysis: # – Af
        Structural change: $X_1 - X_2 \,\text{---}\, X_1 - do + X_2$

The word boundary transformation applies to Tree 7 yielding Tree 8.[6]

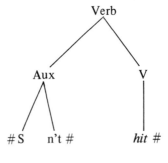

Tree 8

Rule 21' then applies to Tree 8, inserting the empty *do* between the word boundary and S, producing Tree 9.

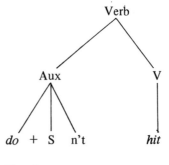

Tree 9

After the application of morphophonemic rules Tree 9 would surface as

... *doesn't hit* ...

59

If Rule 17 had applied instead of Rule 16, Rule 21' would still have been called upon and the resultant string would have been

... does hit ...

1.2. *Tagmemic objections.* Consider now the reactions of three tagmemic authors to this general approach. These reactions are to be found in two papers, one by Longacre entitled "A hierarchical look at the English verb Phrase" (forthcoming) and one by Kenneth and Evelyn Pike entitled "Rules as components of tagmemes in the English verb phrase" (1974). These objections suggest certain candidate constraints upon underlying structure in tagmemic description.

Both papers vigorously reject Chomsky's solution. They do not view Chomsky's solution as a consistent result of an alternative perspective which might be allowed within tagmemics. Rather, Chomsky's result is held to be incompatible with tagmemics on theoretical grounds. It lacks systematic coherence with tagmemics. It is reasonable, then, to expect that the reasons for this rejection may tell us something important about tagmemic constraints on underlying structure.

There appear to be three basic tagmemic objections to Chomsky's analysis of the English auxiliary: 1) The analysis violates the integrity of the word as a unit, 2) The analysis violates the constituent relationships of affix to word and of word to phrase within the hierarchy, and 3) The analysis does not associate the auxiliary closely enough with the verb. The third objection probably does not apply to Chomsky's original analysis, but rather to other versions in which Tree 10 is a frequently encountered tree structure.

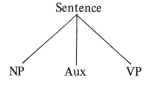

Tree 10

The chief offender appears to be Rule 10.

10.   Aux --- → C (M) (*have* + en) (*be* + ing) (*be* + en)[7]

With the exception of the element C which represents two morphemes, and the element M which represents a substitution class of modal verbs, the

elements in Rule 10 correspond quite well to the morphemes of Pike and
Pike's analysis. The integrity of morphemes has been respected. There is no
complaint in this regard. What appears to be at stake are two highly
interrelated tagmemic constraints upon underlying structure.[8]

Constraint 1.   Whatever is a unit in surface structure must be represented
                as a unit in underlying structure.
Constraint 2.   Whatever hierarchical groupings are present in surface
                structure must also be present in underlying structure.

Rule 10 clearly violates Constraint 1 with respect to words in surface
structure. Rule 10 contains no direct representations of words. Rules 20 and
21 are required as supplements to Rule 10. Only after the application of
Rules 20 and 21 are words directly represented in derived structure. It is also
clear that Rule 10 violates Constraint 2. None of the groupings represented in
Rule 10 ever occur in surface structure. Indeed, it is for this reason that Rules
20 and 21 are obligatory.

Chomsky's motivations for this analysis are quite consistent with the view
that the underlying structure is a rational, uniform presentation of
grammatical relations.[9] From this point of view *have + en*, for example, *is*
conceived of as an underlying unit of sorts, one to which one could also
assign a meaning such as 'perfect'. Surface structure has a discontinuous
representation of the perfect; the underlying, rational representation is
continuous.

Chomsky thus has two levels of representation, one concerned with
function and one concerned with form.[10] In tagmemic terms Chomsky has
split form and meaning and resorted to transformations to link them back
together. The distinction between deep and surface structure that grew out of
this split has at times been considered one of the major achievements of
transformational grammar.[11] From a tagmemic point of view it constitutes a
violation of Constraint 3[12].

Constraint 3.   Wherever a unit is posited, both form and meaning must be
                given as components of that unit.

1.3. *A tagmemic view of the English auxiliary.* Pike and Pike's contribution
goes well beyond mere criticism of other views. One of the most interesting
aspects of their analysis is their introduction of rules as emic features of
tagmemes. The fact that rules in a tagmemic description are subordinate to
units is clearly apparent both in the exposition and in the formulaic
representation of the analysis. The active indicative nonemphatic verb phrase

is given the following representation.

ActIndicNonemphVP = ± iMar: MoV ± n₁ Mar: < not > ± j *Mar: CRV*
± k Mar: State V + / − n₂ Mar: EmptyV + m Nuc: ActIndicMnV

The symbols, i, n_1, j, k, n_2, and m are *rule indices* and operate as follows:

i   suppresses the inflection of a following verb stem.
n_1 triggers a rule for placement of the negative morpheme.
j   governs the choice of the participial form <-N> on the following verb stem.
k   governs the choice of the <-*ing*> form on the following verb stem.
n_2 refers to a condition governing the choice of the EmptyV. It says to choose EmptyV just in case the only other constituents within the verb phrase are *not* and the main verb. Otherwise the EmptyV cannot be chosen.
m   refers to a rule which places the tense morpheme on the first verb stem in the verb phrase.

The rules to which these rule indices refer are given only in prose. Corresponding to rule indices i, j, k, and m, are squarebracketed reminders in word level formulae which alert the reader to the various possible rules which may influence the form of the word level structure in question.[13]
    The modal verb has the following word level structure.

MoV = + Nuc:MoRt + Mar: [*m*]+/− Tense

Once one has chosen MoV, it is necessary to choose both a nucleus and a margin. The filler for the margin, [m]+/− Tense may be read, "if [m] is present, choose tense, otherwise omit tense." It is not altogether clear what circumstances govern the minus option for Tense within MoV, since subordinate structures which have no tense (*He told me to go*) also appear to reject modal verbs (**He told me to must go*). If it is true that the minus option is never exercised, this formula is confusing to the reader as it stands.
    The formula for the Current Relevance Verb (CRV) contains one option not present in the formula for MoV.

CRV = + Nuc:<*have*> [i] -/+ Mar:[m]+/-Tense

If MoV is chosen at phrase level, the rule feature [i] associated with MoV governs a minus choice in the margin of CRV.

The formula for the StateV has more than one possible expansion of its margin.

StateV = + Nuc:<*be*>[i]–/+ Mar:[m]+/– Tense
$$[j]+/-<-N>,$$

The index [i] controls a minus option on the margin as a whole. This insures that the stem form, *be*, will appear following a modal verb, as in *He must be coming*. The indices [m] and [j] each control a plus option. These two options are nonorthogonally related to one another in the sense that there will never be two plus options within a given margin of the StateV. The index [m] insures that Tense will be chosen when StateV stands first within the verb phrase. The index [j] insures that the participial form will be chosen when StateV follows CRV within the verb phrase.

The empty verb and the main verb share the same set of possible inflections. In addition to those which occur with StateV, these two verbs both have <–*ing*> as their inflection whenever they occur following StateV.

EmptyV = + Nuc: <*do*> [i] –/+ Mar: [m] +/– Tense
$$[j] +/- <-N>$$
$$[k] +/- <-ing>$$

ActIndicMnV = + Nuc:MnVRt [i] –/+ Mar: [m] +/– Tense
$$[j] +/- <-N>$$
$$[k] +/- <-ing>$$

We will now attempt part of a sample derivation of a verb phrase. Since the rules are given in prose, we will also attempt to formalize some of them. The underlying structure to which the rules first apply is the full phrase level formula.

± i Mar:MoV ± n_1 Mar: <*not*> ± j Mar:CRV ± k Mar:StateV +/–n_2
Mar:EmptyV + m Nuc:ActIndicMnV

Step 1 involves the exercise of optional choices marked ± in the underlying structure. Items marked +/– are treated as + options at this stage of the derivation. The following is a possible option.

Step 1:
j Mar:CRV k Mar:StateV +/–n_2 Mar:EmptyV m Nuc:ActIndicMnV

Step 2 involves checking the derived string against condition n_2 which states that the EmptyV is obligatory in verb phrases which otherwise contain only the negative tagmeme and the main verb. In all other cases the EmptyV is deleted. Two strictly ordered rules appear to be required:

Do Keep[14]
SD: ActIndicNonemphVP[, n_1 Mar: $<$ not $>$, $+/$-n_2 , Mar:EmptyV X]
         1   2   3   4
SC: 1 , 2 , ϕ , 4
CA: obligatory

Do Keep deletes the occurrence conditions on the Empty V in all environments in which the EmptyV survives.

Do Delete

SD: X , $+/-n_2$ Mar:EmptyV , Y
     1   2   3
SC: 1 , ϕ , 3
CA: obligatory

Do Delete deletes the EmptyV tagmeme in all instances in which its occurrence conditions have not been deleted. Note here that it would have been simpler as far as the technical use of transformational rules is concerned to write a rule to insert the empty verb in the one environment in which it is appropriate than it is to develop the empty verb in the phrase level formula and then delete it in all environments *except* the one appropriate environment in which it is to survive. It is curious that n_2 is even called an insertion rule (Pike - Pike 1974: 184) since n_2 clearly must operate as a deletion rule as long as the EmptyV is already expanded in the phrase level formula, (Pike - Pike 1974:182). If EmptyV had been omitted from the phrase level formula, n_2 could have been formulated as an insertion rule something like the following.

Do Insertion
SD: ActIndicNonemphVP[n_1 Mar: $<$ *not* $>$, m Nuc:ActIndicMnV]
                       1   2
SC: 1 , Mar:EmptyV , 2
CA: obligatory

This single rule would then have replaced both Do Keep and Do Delete. The reason for making this observation is not to suggest a change in the analysis, but rather to bring attention to evidence regarding the nature of priorities in the motivation of analyses within tagmemics. In a theory which places priority upon the rules, one would clearly choose Do Insertion rather than the ordered combination of Do Keep and Do Delete, other things being equal. In a theory wich places priority upon the tool value of units in hierarchy, however, EmptyV belongs in the underlying structure in spite of the added cost of the rules which ensues. As a part of the verb phrase formula, EmptyV is a visual reminder of the fact that it has a place within the total structure of the verb phrase.

The fact that Pike and Pike have posited EmptyV as a unit in underlying structure raises another question. It brings Constraint 1 (that units in surface structure be represented as units in underlying structure) into apparent conflict with Constraint 3 (that both form and meaning be given as components of units in underlying structure). If the EmptyV is indeed meaningless it would be a violation of Constraint 3 to include it as a unit in underlying structure. Note, however, that the reason for excluding it would be a semantic reason, not a formal, grammatical one. In surface structure the EmptyV always combines with some meaningful category such as tense and thus, *as a word* is surely a unit in surface structure. The fact that EmptyV is included in underlying structure is consistent with an additional constraint which might be expressed somewhat as follows:

Constraint 4.   Grammatical form takes priority over lexical or sememic relations in the organization of underlying structure.

There are a number of other decisions that appear to support Constraint 4 as relevant to actual tagmemic practice. If, for example, sememic considerations were allowed to take priority in the analysis of the English auxiliary, the organization of underlying structure would be radically different from that which Pike and Pike present. The tense morpheme, for example, has a sememic function which relates to the clause as a whole. Its sememic function is clearly a clause level function. Sememic facts would dictate an organization in which tense is a clause level constituent. Grammatically, however, tense is a morpheme bound to a verb stem at word level. In the analysis under consideration, grammatical form clearly takes priority. Step 2 yields the following result.

Step 2: j Mar:CRV k Mar:StateV m Nuc:ActIndicMnV

Step 3 involves the transfer of the affix governing rule indices from the tagmemes with which they were chosen to the tagmemes they ultimately control. This is the analog of Chomsky's Rule 20. Step 3 involves a number of rules, the first two of which appear to be strictly ordered.

Tense Move 1
SD: ActIndicNonemphVP [X: , Y Z , m , Nuc:ActIndicMnV]
           1   2   3   4
SC: 1 , 3 + 2 , 4
CA: X is a single slot and is not null, obligatory

Tense Move 2
SD: X , m , Nuc: , ActIndicMnV Y
     1   2   3   4
SC: 1 , 3 , 2 + 4
CA: obligatory

Tense Move 1 and Tense Move 2 could have been combined into a single rule if m had been allowed to float free at the beginning of the verb phrase. The rule that would have been required in this event would have been the following:

Tense Move 3[15]
SD: X , m , Y: , Z
     1   2   3   4
SC: 1, 3 , 2 + 4
CA: Y is a single slot within VP, obligatory

Pike and Pike realized the economy that this placement would make possible but they still rejected this solution (1974:185). This solution runs afoul of constraints on unit and hierarchy in underlying structure. The element, m, is only a rule index. It is not a tagmeme with a function on phrase level. It does not even qualify as a unit. Since it is not a unit it must be carried as a feature of something that is a unit. Moreover, it is an obligatory index within the verb phrase and thus can attach only to an obligatory unit of the verb phrase. Since grammatical organization takes priority over sememic organization the index cannot be attached to the verb phrase as a whole, but must be attached to some constituent of the verb phrase. The only obligatory constituent unit of the verb phrase is the main verb. As a consequence, m is attached to the main verb. The fact that these considerations forced the present analysis even at the cost of added complexity in the rules provides evidence of the existence of some constraint on underlying structure such as the following.

66

Constraint 5.   Tagmemic underlying structure consists exclusively of
units. Rules, relations, classes, etc. are regarded as
components or emic features of units and not as units in
their own right.

The second part of step 3 involves moving the rule features i, j, and k to the
verbs which follow their respective tagmemes.

Affix Feature Move
SD: X , a , Mar:F Y SL: , Z
   1 2   3   4
SC: 1 , 3 , 2 + 4
CA: F is a single filler; Y is either Mar: <not> or is null; SL is a single
slot; a is either i, or j, or k; obligatory.

Step 3 yields the following.

Step 3   Mar: m + CRV   Mar: j + StateV   Nuc: k + ActIndicMnV

Step 4 involves the expansion of word level structure one at a time under the
constraints imposed upon them by the rule features which have just been
moved into position in Step 3. As a representative example, consider the
expansion of CRV.

+ Nuc: < *have* > [i] –/+ Mar: [m]+/– Tense

The margin of CRV contains three options. If the rule index of CRV is [i],
the minus option applies to the margin as a whole. If the rule index |[i] is
absent, the margin is retained. If the rule feature of CRV is [m], the filler for
the margin is Tense. If neither [i] nor [m] were present, the margin would be
retained but Tense would be deleted. As the description now stands this is
not likely to occur. In the derivation which we are now following [m] is
present and so Tense is retained. Continuing in the same way, Step 4
ultimately yields the following.

Nuc: < *have* > Mar: Tense Nuc: < *be* > Mar: <–N> Nuc:MnVRt Mar: <–*ing* >

Further rules which are also given by Pike and Pike lead to the generation of
some phrase such as *has been hitting*.
    The analytic decisions made by Pike and Pike in the analysis of the English
auxiliary have suggested the following as candidate constraints upon

underlying structure in tagmemics.
1. Whatever is a unit in surface structure must be represented as a unit in underlying structure.
2. Whatever hierarchical groupings are present in surface structure must also be present in underlying structure.
3. Wherever a unit is posited, both form and meaning must be given as components of that unit.
4. Grammatical form takes priority over lexical or sememic relations in the organization of underlying structure.
5. Tagmemic underlying structure consists exclusively of units. Rules, relations and classes are regarded as components or emic features of units and not as units in their own right.

One crucial article such as the one discussed above may furnish a good starting point in formulating such constraints but it can hardly count as conclusive proof of the relevance or correctness of these constraints for tagmemics in general. We turn now to a consideration of these constraints within a wider context of tagmemic research.

1.4. Constraints upon underlying structure and the major tagmemic tenets.
If the constraints which have been put forward to account for certain analytical decisions in Pike and Pike's analysis of the English verb phrase are deeply motivated within tagmemics, they should at least be in harmony with the major tenets of tagmemics. The list of tenets has appeared in a number of places and constitutes a very helpful characterization of tagmemics. See, for example, Pike, 1964b, 1964c; Klammer 1971: 25-34.

The tenets of tagmemics center around four major concepts: *Unit, hierarchy, context,* and *perspective.* The notion of unit is central to the discussion of each of the four concepts. The notion of rule is relatively peripheral by comparison. Underlying structure consists of units. Hierarchy is a principle according to which units are arranged in underlying structure. Context relates to certain limiting characteristics of units in underlying structure. Perspective involves alternative ways of viewing units in underlying structure.

The tenets which relate to the concept of *unit* are concerned with what a nonnative participant in a given culture needs to know about a unit before he can utilize it in a way acceptable to native participants. In tagmemic terms, this information constitutes the definition of a unit, and it includes not only that which is required to identify the unit in contrast to all other units but it also includes a specification of all variants of the unit, the contexts which control the occurrence of these variants, and a specification of the total distribution of the unit. One constraint upon tagmemic grammars is that they provide this kind of unit definition. Where well-defined units are in focus (and in a tagmemic description they generally are) the tenets related to unit have some clear consequences for the organization of the description. It involves grouping elements of the description so as to present coherent definitions of the units under consideration. Elements of form and meaning which relate to a given unit should occur together in the description and not scattered throughout the description as is often the case where rules are in focus and emphasis is placed upon coherent statements of regularity. The price of this emphasis is the fragmenting and scattering of rule-like regularities throughout the description. Where rules are used explicitly, as in Jacobs - Longacre (1967), they are clustered around the units to which they apply. Rules are sometimes even repeated when they apply to more than one unit.

One may choose to focus upon units or upon rules within a description. A difference in choice at this point leads to great differences in the organization of the grammar and ultimately leads to radical differences in the mode of argumentation used in getting from the data to a description. Transformational grammar and tagmemics represent almost paradigm examples of opposite choices in this regard. Constraints 1, 3, and 5 are quite in harmony with the choice that tagmemics makes at this point.

The tenets which relate to the concept of *hierarchy* are concerned with the way in which larger units are made up of smaller units. From a tagmemic point of view, there are three different ways in which larger units are made up of smaller units. Units are structured phonologically, grammatically, and lexically (or sememically). A focus upon hierarchy is consistent with a focus upon units. It provides further obstacles to any coherent general statement of the rules. The problem of discontinuous or misplaced constituents[16] continues to be a severe one within a tagmemic frame of reference largely because it constitutes a major exception to hierarchy in surface structure. This set of tenets is quite in harmony with Constraint 2.

Within a transformational grammar, the base rules assign a hierarchical constituent structure to sentences on the basis of underlying semantic and syntactic relations. Where these underlying relations come in conflict with the organization of actual sentences in surface structure, the underlying representation has tended to reflect the deeper relationships. The function of transformations is to relate these underlying representations to the surface relationships. The problems of interrupted hierarchy, misplaced constituents, structural ambiguity of surface structures, and meaning relations between structurally distinct surface structures are problems that have been approached in terms of transformational rules. Indeed, it is these problems that have so convincingly motivated the use of such rules in general. Within tagmemics there has long been a resistance to the use of derivations and rules simply for the sake of describing the end points of a static system. There is an unwillingness to incorporate rules which might be objected to as pseudo-historical statements. The cost of this has been that as far as the transformationalist is concerned these problems simply remain unsolved within tagmemics. The tagmemic choice at this point, however, is quite in harmony with Constraints 2, 4, and 5.

The tenets which relate to the concept of context are concerned with three kinds of relationships involving units: the relationship of form and meaning, relationships involving change, and the relationship of a unit to its universe of discourse. Constraint 3 is directly supported by the tagmemic view of the relationship of form and meaning. A unit is a tightly bound composite of form and meaning. Neither form nor meaning is profitably studied without reference to the other.

The tenets which relate to the concept of *context* are concerned with the relationship of the observer to the data. Within tagmemics there are no facts without an observer. One of the basic reasons for the importance of units within tagmemics stems from the unitizing ability of human observers. Although the stimuli which form the basis of sense experience are at least as continuous as they are discrete, human beings perceive their experiences as consisting of units. According to tagmemics, an observer may choose to look at a unit in any one of three ways. One can view units simply as entities (particles). One can view a unit as an entity changing over time (wave). One can view a unit as a point in a matrix of relationship (field). Ultimately each of the three perspectives relates to units. Regardless of perspective it is units that are in focus. This set of tenets is quite in harmony with Constraint 5.

1.5 *Longacre and hierarchy in underlying structure.* Longacre (1960) insists that the layering assigned to units in underlying structure should be significant (86). He proposes that binary immediate constituent cuts in syntactic analysis should be replaced by cuts which yield functional units in significant relations to one another on a limited number of labeled levels. This suggests an addition to Constraint 2 upon underlying structure in tagmemics.

Contraint 2a.   Tagmemic underlying structure is organized into contrastive emic (language-specific levels. Every unit of the description is assigned to a specific level.

Where semantic function and grammatical form provide potentially conflicting motivations for the assignment of a unit to a level, grammatical form apparently wins. Affixes always appear to end up on word level even when their semantic scope includes a whole clause. (See, for example, the past tense morpheme, *—ed*, of *pull-ed* in Table 2 (Longacre 1960:69) as well as the statement "In the Trique verb, word-level tagemmes mark aspect, mood, causative, stative, and resumptive." (Longacre 1960:84).) Longacre is not unaware of the taxonomic nature of this constraint. The concluding section of this article is basically a defense of the use of name labeling and taxonomy in linguistics.

Evidence in support of the relevance of Constraint 2a (or of something like it) within tagmemic analysis can be found in many of Longacre's writings. Longacre's *Grammar discovery procedures*, for example, includes a defense of taxonomy in its introduction (1964a: 10-11) and then dedicates each of its four chapters to procedures for grammatical analysis of one of the four levels (clause, phrase, word, sentence) represented in Table 2 of Longacre (1960).

Longacre (1964b) continues the characteristically heavy emphasis upon hierarchy and the correlation of units and levels. A great deal of productive work has been done in phonology from the particle point of view, but in Longacre's opinion the particle point of view has been considerably less helpful in grammatical analysis and has been largely replaced by "a string-oriented approach in which hierarchy is a primitive of structure"(10). Extrapolating, Longacre expects the study of lexicon to require a field-oriented approach.

Two of the four fundamental insights of tagmemics mentioned by Longacre (1965a: 65) have to do with constraint 2a. "Four fundamental insights of tagmemics are the correlativity of function and set, the search for constructions of maximum relevance, the emphasis upon explicit, systemic hierarchy, and the concept of relatedness in logical space (with transformation only one of the possible parameters which relate constructions)." Later in the article (1965a: 72) Longacre makes the importance of hierarchy even clearer. "The notion of structural levels arranged in explicit systemic hierarchy is another basis concept of tagmemics. Syntagmeme and level are correlative concepts: the former is defined (as already noted) as a functionally contrastive string on a given level of hierarchical structuring. This correlativity of syntagmeme and level must be added to the correlativity of function and set (within the tagmeme) and the correlativity of tagmeme and syntagmeme. Only by positing systemic levels in the structuring of a given language can constructions of maximum relevance be obtained."

The methodological importance of working back and forth between unit and level within hierarchy is stressed in Longacre (1970b). "In setting up a hierarchical system, we must work back and forth between levels and units on levels. To define levels wholly in terms of units with neatly descending hierarchy results in incoherent, nondistinctive units ... On the other hand, to define levels over-much in terms of an etic idea of what the units on a level look like is to obtain levels that do not make a plausible hierarchical scheme. We must meet the twin demands of plausible, contrasting units and plausible, contrasting levels" (1970b:189). Possibly the best treatment of hierarchy from Longacre's point of view is that of Longacre (1973).

1.6 *Deep grammar in tagmemic underlying structure.* More recently, in articles coauthored with Ballard and Conrad, Longacre has expanded his view of underlying structure. He now includes a representation of deep grammar alongside the surface-grammar representation which has been stanard in earlier works in tagmemics. This approach is exemplified in Longacre (1972) as well. Judging from what has been done thus far, deep grammar in tagmemics consists of a representation of relationships between clauses in terms of a certain logical notation.[17] Tagmemic deep grammar is not an abstract representation of semantic or syntactic relations from which a surface representation is derived through the application of rules. Rather, it is a kind of logical cross-classification of surface structures in terms of the deep-structure relations that they can express. It represents a partial relaxation of our putative Constraints 3, 4, and 5.

It represents a relaxation of Constraint 3 because it amounts to a factoring out of surface grammar certain meaningful relations which are represented in deep grammar. In practice, deep and surface grammar representations are located in close physical proximity within the description, yet it is still true that some components of meaning are abstracted from the actual units of surface grammar by this approach.

It represents a partial relaxation of Constraint 4 in offering two parallel principles of organizing underlying structures. It is now just as possible to classify surface grammatical forms in an outline which takes its major headings from the relations of deep grammar as it is to classify deep grammar relations in an outline which takes its major headings from the formal structures of surface grammar. The reverse index of Ballard *et al.* (1970a: 111-114) actually accomplished just this. One can enter the grammar with certain abstract semantic relations and exit with a specific set of grammatical forms just as easily as one can enter with a grammatical form and exit with a set of deep-grammar interpretations.[18]

It represents a relaxation of Constraint 5 in the sense that the deep-grammar relations are probably not units and are not composed of units in anything like the normal tagmemic sense of the notion *unit.* Yet it seems appropriate to hold that these deep grammatical representations do belong to underlying structure in Longacre's version of tagmemics. It remains to be seen what impact this approach will have upon future developments within tagmemics as a whole.

1.7 *'Case' in tagmemic underlying structure.* The need for role relations in underlying structure has long been recognized within tagmemics. At least as early as 1954, Pike was distinguishing between actor-as-subject and recipient of action-as-subject (Pike 1954: 131; 1967: 576-77, 607). This emphasis upon the need to recognize situational roles as distinct from grammatical roles is enlarged upon in Pike (1964) and was developed at length in Becker (1967) as an aspect of a grammatical unit at clause level. Figure 1 is from Becker (1967: 6, 14).

	Grammar	Lexicon
Form	A (e.g., Subject)	C (e.g., Noun Phrase)
Meaning	B (e.g., agent)	D (e.g., single male human, etc.)

Figure 1
Aspects of grammatical unit (Becker 1967: 6, 14).

The entry for cell B, Grammatical Meaning, within noun phrase of the clause level would be the tagmemic analogue of case in transformational grammar.

Platt (1971) critically examines Becker (1967) and Fillmore (1968) with a view toward constructing consistent criteria for grammatical meanings in English. Becker's study was largely restricted to the English subject tagmeme. Platt attempts to cover all nominal-clause-level tagmemes in English. He speaks of grammatical meaning as a kind of deep structure within tagmemics (1971: 151).

Pike's emphasis upon situational role is also reflected in Wise (1968). (See especially page 24 of the 1971 edition.) Wise prefers a different labeling of the axes than that used by Becker.

	Function	Manifestation
Grammatical Unit	A (e.g., Subject)	C (e.g., Noun Phrase)
Lexemic	B (e.g., agent)	D (e.g., single male human, etc.)

Figure 2
Aspects of the tagmeme (Wise 1971: 24).

A fuller development of this approach within tagmemics may be found in Klammer (1971: 96-108) which is one of the first presentations of what has since become known as the 9-box tagmeme. Klammer also gives a good account of the developments that led to the 9-box tagmeme (1971: 87-102).

Tagmeme	Function	Class & System	Manifesting Item & Variants
G (Grammatical Tagmeme)	Subject	a. Class NP b. System + sg., etc.	John
L (Lexemic Tagmeme)	Agent	a. Class Person b. System + Anim + Hum + Male + Young etc.	John Doe III, he, John, the boy, my friend John, The one with blond hair, Jack, etc.
P (Phonological Tagmeme)	E.g., Bearer of primary stress	a. Class Syllable b. System	/jan/ , /jon/, etc.

Figure 3
Nine-box display of one system of clause-level tagmemes (after Klammer (1971: 97)).

It was essentially this latter view of the tagmeme that formed the basis for the development of role as a 'box 4' function in Hale (1972, 1973a, 1973b).

In Cook (1971) the suggestion was made that case grammar be adopted as a deep structure for tagmemics. Fillmore (1968: 88) had previously recognized the close relationship between the underlying representations of case grammar and tagmemic formulae.

Hale, stimulated by Pike, attempted to systematize the set of role relations at clause level by factoring out such non-relational components as animate and inanimate which distinguish between cases in most systems of role relations and by positing a closed set of relations in terms of which clause types could be defined. The closed set first proposed consisted of three role relations: actor, undergoer, and site. (Site is now referred to in Pike - Pike 1973 as Scope.) This set of three roles combine to yield an etic set of eight clause types as shown in Figure 4.

74

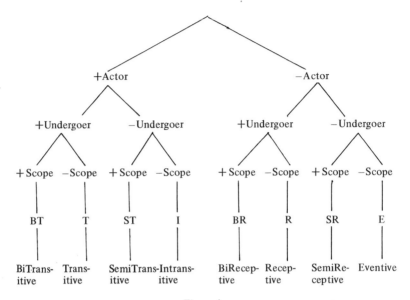

Figure 4
The transivity system (etic) as defined by role features (modified from Hale 1973a: 8 and Pike and Pike 1973, chapter 4).

The features with plus and minus coefficients represent roles within the nucleus of the clause. The labels at the ends of the branches are names for the various combinations of the rules that occur in clause types. Thus, a clause which has an actor and an undergoer but no scope is labeled transitive.

On this view actors can be either animate as in

John hit Bill

or inanimate as in

The plow cleared the snow off the sidewalk.

In the same way undergoers

John hit Bill
John hit the desk

and scopes

John gave the book to Bill
John put the book on the shelf

can be either animate or inanimate. For a lengthy description of the clause structure of a language from this point of view see Watters (1973). See also Bandhu (1973); Taylor (1973); Hale - Watters (1973).

Longacre (1973) appears to prefer a list of roles very much like that which is developed in chapter 8 of Grimes (to appear). Hale has attempted to relate the etic three-role system of Hale (1973a) to the more finely subdivided system in Grimes in Hale - Manandhar (1973). Pike has objected to this attempt on pedagogical and heuristic grounds.

2. RULES IN TAGMEMICS

Tagmemics and transformational grammar can be contrasted in their use of rules and units as descriptive devices. Units are central to any tagmemic description.[19] The overwhelming preference in the work of Pike and Longacre appears to be to account for as much as possible by means of inventories of units interrelated in terms of class membership, occurrence in sequence, in hierarchy, and in system. What is not conveniently treated in this way may then be treated in terms of rules which in Pike's view are mostly emic freatures of units (Pike - Pike 1974: 175-177). This close association of rules with specific units results in a tendency toward a kind of cyclical application of various rule types which can be seen both in Longacre (1964a: 29) and in Pike - Pike (1974: 187-189). As has been seen in Section 1.3 above, the integrity of units and the direct representation of surface relations between units is preserved in tagmemic underlying structure even at the cost of added complexity in the rules.

There is relatively little in the way of formal definition of rules in tagmemics. Formalism is always viewed as secondary to the goals of description. It is never an end in itself. Pike's most eloquent statement to this effect is Pike (1973). The choice of a formalism must be dictated by considerations outside the formalism. This view is also clearly shared by Chomsky (1957), where a choice between alternative forms of grammar is required to be motivated by empirical considerations. The difference between the two is best understood in terms of what is more basic in linguistic description, units or rules. The formalisms of tagmemics are those that highlight units. Those of transformational grammar are those that highlight rules. It is quite obvious that a trimodal, unit-oriented, multiple-perspective view of tagmemics with its openness to all manner of contextual, nonverbal elements is more difficult to formalize as a coherent system than a uni-modal, rule-oriented view that largely disregards nonlinguistic context. In face of the usual sneer that tagmemics is "not a theory" since no one has succeeded in formalizing it, one might suggest that the more nearly formal theories such as transformational grammar have thus far failed to accommodate certain facts about units, hierarchy, trimodal structure, context, and observer perspective. As it stands, one must either place priority upon formalism and choose the best formal theory available, even though it fails to accommodate many relevant facts or else one must place priority upon the kinds of facts that have been relevant and helpful in the analytic process and simply recognize that as yet no formal theory accounts for them all. In this kind of a situation sneers are ill-advised.

2.1 *Rules in Longacre.* In *Grammar Discovery Procedures* (1964a: 24-32) Longacre distinguishes three different kinds of operations which are involved in the generative interpretation of a tagmemic grammar. Although they are referred to as "rewrite operations", they are not language-specific rules but are rather general instructions on how to read a tagmemic description as a generative device. Generation starts with a set of tagmemic formulae which are not viewed as rules but rather as "map-like summaries of constructions" (Longacre 1964a: 24). Three operations, R,P, and E, are applied to these formulae in the generation of language material.[20]

In performing operation R (reading), one chooses to retain or omit a tagmeme marked ±. In certain instances, operation R assigns a value to a superscript ^{n} associated with a repeatable or iterative tagmeme within a formula. Superscript numbers may appear in the formulae whenever there is an upper limit to repetition or iteration. Where superscript numbers appear, one may allow the tagmeme so marked to occur any number of times equal to or less than the superscript number. One may start with a formula such as the following (Longacre 1964a: 86).

$$\text{Coordinate I: } + H_1 \ (\pm H_2)^n + C + H_3$$

If one chooses to omit the tagmeme marked ± in this formula, one obtains the reading, $H_1 \ C \ H_3$. If one chooses to retain the ± tagmeme, one must also assign a value (1 or greater) to the superscript ^{n} associated with it. Where n = 2, the reading obtained would be $H_1 \ H_2 \ H_2 \ C \ H_3$.

In performing operation P (permutation), one chooses a possible ordering for the tagmemes of a given construction. This operation is controlled by language-specific rules which accompany the formula within the grammar. In Longacre's example these rules appear in English prose (Longacre 1964a: 26-27).

Intransitive Clause: $+ P_1 + S \pm L^2 \pm T^2$

Ordering rules: (1) One symbol at a time may be moved to the left of P^{21}.

(2) Contiguous LT may vary to TL, but neither may occur bracketed by a cluster of the other (e.g., TLT and LTLT do not occur).

The statement of these rules is not altogether clear. Longacre gives 28 of the 34 possible permutations. In the samples given, the predicate tagmeme occurs only in the first (leftmost) or second position within the clause. The ordering rule (1) thus appears to apply only once to any given clause. The second rule appears to be a special permutation rule which applies only to a substring of the form LLT. The permutation does not apply to a substring of the form LLT because the resultant string would consist of a T bracketed by two L tagmemes. The permutation does not apply to LTT because the resultant string would consist of an L bracketed by two T tagmemes. For similar reasons this permutation does not apply to LLTT. What Longacre does not point out here is that his two rules are ordered. He does have LPSTL. This string derives from an underlying PSLLT. Rule 1 must apply first yielding LPSLT. Only then can rule 2 apply to yield LPSTL. If we are safe in assuming that the central devices of a theory will be the first to receive formal treatment, the situation at this point in Longacre's thinking lends support to the view that units are central and rules peripheral since units (syntagmemes) are given a kind of formal representation while rules are not.

In performing operation E (exponence), one replaces a given tagmeme with a formula or a lexical item. Operation E is analogous to the expansion of a node by a role in the base component of a transformational grammar. The fact that Longacre deems it necessary to specify operation E at all may be an indication that he does not view his formulae as rules in their own right. Once operation E has been performed, the cycle of operations R, P, and E is performed again on any formulae which occur as exponents or constituents of the unit under attention. For an attempt to formalize these operations as rewrite rules, see Becker (1967: 49-54).

In "Transformational parameters in tagmemic field structures" (1965b) Longacre makes use of transformational rules as a means of indicating explicit relationships among clause types. The emphasis here is still upon syntagmemes as units. Rules are considered helpful for showing relationships between the various grammatical constructions of a language, but are less basic than units represented as syntagmemes.[22] One example of such a rule is the rule used to describe the relationship between the intransitive clause in Zoque and a transitive clause derived from an underlying intransitive clause by the addition of a benefactive object.

(3) $+ P_i:V_i \pm S:NP_1 \dashrightarrow + P_t:V\text{-hay}(_t) \pm S:NP_1 \pm O:NP_2$

(where P_i = intransitive predicate; S = subject; P_t = transitive predicate; O = object; V_i = intransitive verb; V–hay = transitive verb formed by adding –hay benefactive; and NP = noun phrase, with subscripts keeping track of identity of phrases in the transformation.)

Longacre's approach to transformational rules integrates well with the tagmemic view of field structure. A system of basic clause types in a language such as Zoque can be represented by means of a diagram such as the one in Figure 5.

	Nontransitive	Intransitive	Transitive	Ditransitive Referential	Ditransitive Causative
Declarative	X	X	X	X	X
Subordinate	X	X	X	X	X
Interrogative	X	X	X	X	X
Imperative		X	X	X	X

Figure 5
Zoque Clause Types

Rule 3 applies to basic clauses in the intransitive column and produces clauses which belong in the transitive column. Derivation of clauses from type to type within a clause type matrix can be very extensive. See, for example, Watters (1973: 151).

A more basic use of rules is to be found in Jacobs - Longacre (1967). In this article tagmemic formulae are not required to bear the total descriptive load. Formulae are supplemented by rules. Neither formulae nor rules are intended to operate alone. In keeping with the view that units take priority over rules[23], rules are associated with particular constructions. The basic contrastive syntagmemes are specified by the formulae. Constraints on cooccurrence, on exponence, and on ordering are given by the rules. Of the thirty-three different verb phrase syntagmemes distinguished by Jacobs and Longacre, a special set of rules is given for each of eleven syntagmemes. For an additional eight syntagmemes, cross reference is made to various of these special rule sets. In addition to the special rule sets, there is a set of general rules which apply to any verb syntagmeme within their respective domains. The article is organized into five major sections, one for each set of syntagmemes under consideration: I. Verb Phrases, II. Noun Phrases, III. Prepositional Phrases, IV. Other Phrases, V. Clauses. Each section (except III and IV for which there are no general rules) begins with a discussion of the general rules which apply as relevant to all the syntagmemes of the section. Following the general rules comes a presentation of each phrase or clause syntagmeme together with the special rules that go with it. Rules are thus interleaved with syntagmemic formulae. Even the general rules are general only with respect to a given construction type. This organization leads to some difficulty for the reader. One encounters the detailed constraints on cooccurrence, permutation, and exponence before one has seen the syntagmemic formulae to which these detailed constraints apply.[24]

Jacobs and Longacre seem torn between a desire to generalize the rules where possible and a desire to keep specific rules and specific constructions together. There are general rules for verb phrases (1967: 326), general rules for noun phrases (1967: 361), and general rules for a certain subset of clauses (1967: 371). But not all rules that could be viewed as general are to be found within the general rules. For example, in verb phrases 111, 112, and 113 the occurrence of aspect 9 controls the choice of subject person C. The rule which dictates the choice of subject person C in verb phrases with aspect 9 is written three times, once for each phrase to which it applies. There are no other verb phrases that allow both a subject person and aspect 9, so there are no other environments in which such a rule would operate. Phrase 601, for example, can have aspect 9, but is has no subject person marker. In any event, the decision to incorporate rules into a tagmemic description does not represent as major a departure from traditional tagmemics as one might think. The rules so incorporated allow the syntagmemic patterns a somewhat simpler formulation. It is still the syntagmemic patterns, however, that are central.

2.2 Rules in Pike - Pike (1974). Jacobs and Longacre treated some rules as general to sets of syntagmemes such as verb phrases or noun phrases. They treated other rules as restricted in application to certain specific syntagmemes such as verb phrase 111 (active intransitive indicative verb phrase). Pike and Pike now explore the possibility of attributing rules to *specific tagmemes* within a syntagmeme.

One of the purposes of this article was to highlight various tagmemic uses of rules. The beginnings of this approach to rules are traceable to early work on tone (Pike 1948: 81-83, 91-92) in which tags or indices were assigned to morphemes to show that they governed certain tone shifts in neighboring words. The grammatical construction chosen as the setting for this particular approach to rules is the English verb phrase.

Rules are classified according to their effect upon neighboring units within a hierarchy of units. There are suppressing rules which govern the minus option on morphemes in neighboring words. There are selection rules which govern the plus option on specific morphemes in neighboring words. There are placement rules which govern a permutation of the indexed tagmeme.

There are rules which are called insertion rules but which actually operate more like conditions for occurrence on the indexed tagmeme. There are also rules for optional occurrence. This amounts very simply to the standard ± index used with optional tagmemes.

Rules are also classified according to the relative position of the indexed tagmeme and the unit which the rule affects. Within a syntagmeme there are progressive rules, which apply to a unit following the indexed tagmeme, regressive rules which apply to a unit which precedes the indexed tagmeme, and there are rules which apply to the indexed tagmeme itself. Within the hierarchy there are multilevel rules which apply to a unit at an adjacent level and there are monolevel rules which apply to a unit at the same level of the hierarchy as the indexed tagmeme.

One might say that at last rules have found their place within tagmemics. They are related to units, to strings, to hierarchy, and (in a different sense of the term, rule, altogether) to field. Their place in each instance is a subordinate one. Rules are emic features of units. They have progressive, regressive or local effects upon strings. They have multilevel or monolevel effects within hierarchy. They relate unit to unit within field.

2.3 *Rules in other tagmemic authors*. It would appear that the more central the position occupied by rules in the thinking of a linguist and in the organization of the grammars that he writes, the more tangential that linguist's position becomes with respect to the main stream of tagmemics as measured by the twelve tenets. Merrifield (1967) is a good example of how a shift of emphasis from units to rules can radically change the organization of the grammar. Merrifield's view is trimodal. His proposal for the form of grammar includes three components, the semantic, the syntactic, and the phonological. For each of these components, Merrifield has both "phrase rules" and "class-membership rules". He distinguishes the two as follows. "Each component of a grammar has rules of at least two sorts: phrase rules and class-membership rules. The latter are distribution classes of the vocabulary (or alphabet) of the component, and the former are the constructions (or patterns) into which they are distributed." (1967: 44-45) Merrifield thus has six sets of rules, four of which are labeled in Figure 6. In addition to these rules Merrifield proposes correspondence rules of two sorts: transformational rules and realization rules. He distinguishes between them as follows. "A transformation places an element in position and a realization rule provides a spelling in terms of the alphabet of the neighboring component." (1967: 52)

Perhaps the crucial point to note is that in giving rules a relatively central position within the grammar, Merrifield dismembers the tagmeme. To have a

	Semantic Component	Syntactic Component	Phonological Component
Phrase Rules	R-rules	P-rules	(not discussed)
Class-membership Rules	K-rules	L-rules	(not discussed)

Figure 6
Rule sets in Merrifield (1967).

tagmeme at all one must label functional relations within a syntagmeme and one must associate these functional labels with category labels representing the appropriate filler classes. Merrifield separates the two in the grammar, thereby destroying the tagmeme as a unit within the grammar.[25] Merrifield's grammar puts functional relations into the semantic component within the R-rules and it puts filler classes into the syntactic component within the P-rules. Merrifield therefore has no unit which one could call a tagmeme. Merrifield would appear then to be moving in a direction which is highly tangential to the mainstream of tagmemics. This, of course, is in no way intended as a negative evaluation of Merrifield's contribution.[26]

Another tagmemic author who has shown considerable interest in rules is Walter A. Cook. Cook (1967: 32-35) appears to treat syntagmemic formulae very much as phrase structure expansion rules in the sense that they may be applied directly in the construction of trees.

Cook (1971) suggests that case frames be used as a deep structure in tagmemic analysis. Details as to the kinds of rules that would be needed and the precise form of a derivation are lacking. What Cook presents, however, suggests that sememic (or lexical) functions such as are found in Becker and Wise's box B and in Pike, and Klammer's box 4 would be assigned to one part of the grammar (developed by a set of realization rules (1971: 6-7) and the grammatical functions such as are found in Becker and Wise's box A and in Pike and Klammer's box 1 would be assigned to another part of the grammar.[27] If this interpretation of Cook is correct, then Cook has given a priority to rules which has split the tagmeme along different lines than Merrifield. The acceptance of the unity of sememic and grammatical components within the tagmeme is not nearly as crucial or as widely accepted within tagmemics as the acceptance of the unity of function and filler-class. Cook's proposal leaves slot and filler intact while splitting off case or role from grammatical function. He splits the 4-box or 9-box tagmeme along modal lines. Furthermore, Cook's organization of the grammar would allow underlying representations to consist of nonunits (such as naked cases) at a certain deep levels of representation. This approach appears to require considerable relaxation of Constraints 2, 3, and 5. Again, these remarks are not intended as a criticism of Cook's work.

For another inventory of rule types within an interesting approach which admits tendencies quite tangential to tagmemics, see Beel (1973: 221-240).

Finally, there is one short article that raises a tagmemic kind of question in a rather untagmemic way. The question is both relevant and interesting. Peter Fries (1970) distinguishes between pernicious and nonpernicious recursion within the generative output of a set of rules. A perniciously recursive set of rules is one which can generate a tree in which a certain node A dominates a string consisting entirely of an identical node A. Fries argues that if perniciously recursive rules are allowed, the system of rules cannot be completely coherent since numerous vacuous ambiguities will be attributed to nonambigious strings. On the other hand, he argues that certain English constructions can only be described by means of perniciously recursive rules. The tagmemic question involved is unstated but clear. Is it possible to give an adequate description of any language using only the descriptive devices afforded by a coherent set of rules? If the answer is negative as Fries' article would suggest, then the subordination of formal rules to more immediately data-oriented concerns may have allowed tagmemicists to avoid many a theoretical blind valley.

NOTES

1 This is a revised and expanded version of a paper presented to the linguistic departments of the University of Michigan and Michigan State University. I wish to express my appreciation to Kenneth L. Pike, Evelyn G. Pike, Ruth M. Brend, Peter H. Fries, and Rachel Costa for helpful discussion of points in the earlier paper. None of them should be held accountable for shortcomings in the present paper. For statements regarding the search for grammatical units in the genesis of tagmemics see Pike (1967a: 5, 287, 1971:8).

2 The basic characteristics of human communicative behavior which are taken as defining tenets of tagmemics have been listed in a number of publications: Pike (1964b; 1964c); Pike - Pike (1973 [chapter 1]: Klammer (1971: 25-34); Hale (1973a: 34-35

3 Chomsky (1962: 129) indicates that in moving away from views such as those of Harris (1951), he has replaced an interest in the analytic procedures which lead to the construction of a grammar with an interest exploring the generative consequences of a grammar employing certain kinds of rules. "Motivated now by the goal of constructing a grammar, instead of a rule of procedure for constructing an inventory of elements, we no longer have any reason to consider the symbols NP, Sentence, VP, and so forth, that appear in these rules to be names of certain classes, sequences, or sequences of classes, and so on, of concrete elements. They are simply elements in a system of representation which has been constructed so as to enable us to characterize effectively the set of English sentences in a linguistically meaningful way." Pike (1967a: 271) takes this statement as an indication that the labeled nodes in the trees generated by a trans- formational grammar are not units in the tagmemic sense of the terms. Postal (1966: 94)

in his review of Longacre (1964) maintains that Chomsky does use many kinds of linguistic units. In answer to Longacre's statement (1964: 14), "Indeed, with increasing animus the transform school of grammar is rejecting the very concept of linguistic units (e.g., morpheme and phoneme) in their activistic preoccupation with rules," Postal says, "It is no accident that Longacre gives no page reference here for the assertion is a complete misrepresentation. In the paper he refers to, Chomsky discusses a theory of grammar which utilizes all of the following kinds of linguistic units: phonetic features, phonetic segments (complexes of phonetic features), phonological features, systematic phonemes (complexes of phonological features), constituents, morphemes (terminal symbols of underlying structures), and formatives (terminal symbols of the ultimate transformationally derived structures." The parties to this quibble clearly have different things in mind when they use the word, *unit*. Many of the items Postal lists as units certainly would not pass for units within tagmemics. Indeed, it is not at all clear how the notion, *unit*, could be defined for transformational grammar in any way remotely comparable to the definition given in tagmemics. In maintaining the position he takes here, Postal either fails to understand what a tagmemicist means by the word, *unit*, or he chooses to equivocate for the sake of spiteful rhetoric.

4 Alternatively, it may substitute *past* for C

5 We are assuming that a pair of permuted elements reattach to the lowest node which dominated them both in the underlying tree. The choice of *–ing* and *hit* as the first pair for permutation is arbitrary. Any other adjacent pair which satisfied the structural description could have been permutated first.

6 As the boundary rule is written, it is not altogether clear what prevents a boundary symbol from being inserted between *S* and *n't*.

7 Chomsky (1957) has two variants of Rule 10. On page 39, the passive (be + en) is included. On page 111, it has been omitted.

8 These constraints may be a bit strong as they stand. Pike - Pike (1974: 178-79) state, "But the theory wants units preserved, where possible, since it claims that if constituents are cavalierly ignored, eventually no theory could survive – not even one of transformational grammar, since it must eventually be based on some 'phrase structure' constituents. The theory wishes hierarchical structure to be preserved, in relation to unit preservation." They state further (1974: 179), "We have rejected that kind of splitting of words which was suggested by Zellig Harris to obtain discontinuous morphemes such as ...*us* ...*us* of *filius bonus* meaning 'male' (see Pike's *Language*, sections 6.54, 7.322 and 7.56)."

9 Longacre now appears to be aware of certain inconsistencies that are inherent in surface structure and of certain advantages of a more abstract deep structure in which the inconsistencies of surface structure can be ignored. See, for example, Longacre, (1973: 152). This awareness has not yet led to any perceptible compromise in matters relating to unit and hierarchy which underly Constraints 1 and 2.

10 Lees (1964: 416-17) makes another interesting observation regarding these two levels. The deeper level approximates an immediate constituent analysis while the shallower approximates a string constituent analysis.

11 Thus Postal (1966:97) states, "The trouble is that Longacre and tagmemics generally have not recognized the fact which is the central insight of transformational grammar, that syntactic structure consists of *two distinct aspects*: *deep structure*, which is highly abstract and relevant to semantic interpretation and in which grammatical relations can be correctly defined, and *surface structure*, an actual bracketing of the sentence relevant to phonetic interpretation alone." (Emphasis is Postal's)

12 A clearer example of this contrast between tagmemics and the early versions of transformational grammar with respect to Constraint 3 can be seen in the way that the two theories deal with the notions of subject and object. Chomsky (1965: 70-72) defines grammatical functions in terms of immediate dominance relationship within phrase markers. Thus the function, subject-of, is defined in terms of the dominance relation,

[NP, S], and the function, object-of, is defined in terms of the dominance relation, [NP, VP]. It is then quite convenient to account for the discrepancy between 'grammatical' subjects and objects and 'logical' subjects and objects by allowing the dominance relations in deep structure to represent those of 'logical' subjects and objects and by allowing the dominance relations in surface structure to represent the functions of 'grammatical' subjects and objects. In a sentence such as *John was hit by Bill, Bill* is 'logical' subject, whereas *John* is both 'grammatical' subject and 'logical' object. It takes two trees to represent these relationships. In this scheme there is no single place in the grammar at which *John* is marked both as grammatical subject and as logical object. One needs a considerable amount of derivational history to determine this. Constraint 3 places tagmemic underlying structure under obligation to treat both kinds of information as relational components of the tagmeme manifested by *John*. Specifically, John's status as 'logical' object is interpreted as a sememic function labeled 'undergoer' and John's status as grammatical subject is interpreted as a grammatical function labelled 'subject'. In standard form this information is represented within the 9-box tagmeme in the following way.

```
S    |  NP  |  John
-----|------|--------
Und  |      |
     |      |
```

13 In the absence of explicit formal rules, the rule indices (other than n_2) given in the phrase level formula may be interpreted as contexts. In the case of n_1 the index triggers a permutation. Otherwise, these indices may simply serve as contexts to which the word formulae look back. These word level formulae can thus be viewed as analogous to context-sensitive expansions with transformational power. If one wished to construct a less redundant grammar and if these indices were viewed as contexts they could simply be omitted since the filler labels in the phrase level formula could perform the same function.
14 The rules are formulated here in a form that approximates that of transformations in a transformational grammar. Labels to the left of a bracket are nodes dominating the string enclosed in brackets. SD is to be read 'structural description'; SC, 'structural change'; and CA, 'conditions for application'. X is a variable. $\emptyset$ is null, replacing a deleted item in the structural description.
15 This formulation of Tense Move 3 assumes that *not* Move has already applied by the time this rule applies.
16 For the term *misplaced constituent* I am indebted to Peter H. Fries.
17 Longacre (1973: 121, 150-60) appears receptive to the use of deep structure throughout the grammatical hierarchy and not just at sentence level. How deep grammar will be represented at other levels remains to be seen.
18 Pike's matrices share this same characteristic. One is allowed to enter a Pike matrix either with a particular form or with a functional parameter. The functional parameters of Pike's matrices are probably no closer to being units in the narrow tagmemic sense than are the logical representations in deep grammar of Ballard - Conrad - Longacre (1971a - 1971b).
19 The distinction between rules and units within tagmemics can be surprising to a transformationalist. From a transformational point of view, a syntactic formula is analogous to a phrase structure expansion rule and can be applied like one. Thus, given a tagmemic formula such as the following

$$Cl_i = +P_i +S \pm L \pm T$$

one would expect that it could be interpreted directly as a rule. The following might be interpreted simply as an alternative notation:

$Cl_i \rightarrow P_i + S$ (L) (T)

One would expect that either of these formal statements could be interpreted as generating sub-trees such as the following:

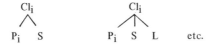

Becker (1967:49), however, suggests a rule which clearly indicates that he, at least, does not regard a syntagmemic formula as a rule in and of itself. The rule Becker suggests is the following:

$$+P_i +S \pm L \pm T \rightarrow \begin{bmatrix} PS \\ PSL \\ PST \\ PSLT \end{bmatrix}$$

20 For other discussions of Longacre's rewrite operations see Becker (1967: 47-49) and Franklin (1971: 33-34).
21 It appears that the original statement of this rule contained a misprint. The type face used for the symbol P in the first ordering rule is that used to refer to the permutation operation. It would seem, however, that P should refer in this instance to the predicate tagmemic of the formula and not to the permutation operation as such.
22 For an explicit statement to this effect, see especially Longacre (1965b: 46). "Grades of transitivity from one on up (intransitive, transitive, and ditransitive) are in partial transformational relationship. Nevertheless, the transitivity scale is more basic than the transformations that partially characterize it. Thus there are verb stems that are inherently intransitive (e.g. *min* 'come'), others that are inherently transitive (*? a? m* 'see'), and still others that are inherently ditransitive (verbs of delivery, such as *ci?* 'give') ... These various verb classes determine kernel clauses on all three grades of transitivity ... Regular transformations derive transitive clauses from intransitive, and ditransitive clauses from transitive. Thus both kernel and derived clauses are found on all three lower grades of transitivity." For extensive examples of a similar approach to the interrelation of clause types, see Watters (1973: 122-184); Bandhu (1973: 46-47; Taylor (1973: 128-158. In each of these studies, however, the rules are given in prose only.
23 For another explicit statement of this priority, see Jacobs - Longacre (1967: 325.
24 There are other difficulties of which the reader should be forewarned. The rules at the beginning of the article are difficult to understand without constant reference to the appendix given on pages 387 and 388, yet no cross-reference is supplied to help the reader. Unexplained conventions provide another source of difficulty. The symbol X appears quite frequently in the general rules for verb phrase but is never really glossed. By comparing rule V12 (1967: 327) with its interpretation (1967: 329) one learns that ~X may be read, "will not cooccur with". Fron this one may surmise that X is to be read, "will cooccur with". The rules make extensive use of English. Permutations are specified only in terms of the order of tagmemes in their output. The difference between obligatory rules such as V3 and optional rules such as V4 and V5 is indicated only in the English wording of the rules themselves ("occur only" vs. "may permute"). The difference between optional and obligatory rules would seem to warrant more attention

than this in a theoretical framework in which obligatory rules are often vulnerable to the charge of being pseudohistory and in which any account of optional rules should be accompanied by some indication of the semantic impact of the option which the rule affords.

25 Merrifield is quite explicit in his discarding of the tagmeme. "Including R-rules in the theory has important implications for the nature of the P-rules as they have been developed to date. The, by now, traditional slot-class notation must be discarded in favor of a simple string of classes. The syntactic development of the Tzotzil verb phrase, for example, begins with the following three P-rules, where parentheses indicate that a constituent is optional to the construction:

(12) VP = (NEG) (ASP) (AUX) NUC (DIR)
      NUC = (PN^1) (PN^2) V (REFL) (PL^2) (PL^3) (PL^1)
      V   = VS (PERF) (REF) (PASS) (MODE)

In discarding the slot-class notation, the concept of 'tagmeme' must go with it. Let me hasten to add that this does not signal any such thing as the expurgation of tagmemic theory from the notion 'grammatical function'. It merely recognizes what Householder noted several years ago, and what anyone who understands tagmemics will readily admit, that in tagmemics slot 'is always a relational expression'. This being the case, it belongs to the semantic component rather than to the syntactic." (1967: 49)

26 For another discussion of Merrifield's rules see Franklin (1971: 35). In fact, Franklin's whole article is a useful supplement to this one. See Franklin for a discussion of Dik's rules within tagmemics. The failure to deal with Dik's contribution here is one of the more unfortunate gaps in the current presentation.

27 See Figures 1, 2, and 3 above for the 4-box and the 9-box representations of the tagmeme.

REFERENCES

Ballard, D. Lee - Robert J. Conrad - Robert E. Longacre
  1971a   "The deep and surface grammar of interclausal relations", *Foundations of Language* 7, 70-118.
  1971b   "More on the deep and surface grammar of interclausal relations", ,Language Data, *Asian-Pacific Series*, Number 1, 1-59.
Bandhu, Churamani
  1973   "Clause patterns in Nepali", *Clause, sentence, and discourse patterns in selected languages of Nepal*, Part II: Clause, ed. by Austin Hale and David Watters (Summer Institute of Linguistics Publications in Linguistics and Related Fields, Publication No. 40) (Norman: The Summer Institute of Linguistics), 1-80.
Becker, Alton L.
  1967   *A generative description of the English subject tagmemes*
          Phd dissertation, university of Michigan.
Bee, Darlene L.
  1973   *Neo-Tagmemics, An integrated approach to linguistic analysis and description* (Ukarumpa: Summer Institute of Linguistics).
Brend, Ruth M. (ed.)
  1972   *Kenneth L. Pike, Selected writings* (The Hague: Mouton).
Chomsky, Noam
  1957   *Syntactic structures* (= *Janua Linguarum*, series minor, 4) (The Hague: Mouton).

87

1962   "A transformational approach to syntax", *Proceedings of the Third Texas Conference on Problems of Linguistic Analysis in English, 1958,* ed. by A.A. Hill (Austin, Texas: The university of Texas), 124-58. (Reprinted in Fodor and Katz, eds., 1964: 211-245.)
1965   Aspects of the theory of Syntax (Cambridge, Mass. M.I.I. Press).
Cook, Walter A.
1964   *On tagmemes and transforms* (Washington, D.C.: Georgetown University Press).
1967   "The generative power of a tagmemic grammar", *(Monograph Series on Languages and Linguistics,* No. 20) (= *Proceedings of the Eighteenth Annual Round Table on Linguistics and Language Studies*) (Washington, D.C.: Georgetown University Press), 27-41.
1971   "Case grammar as a deep structure in tagmemic analysis", *Languages and Linguistics Working Papers* No. 2 (Washington, D.C.: Georgetown University School of Languages and Linguistics), 1-9.
Fillmore, Charles J.
1968   "The case for case", *Universals in linguistic Theory* ed. by Emmon Bach and Robert T. Harms (New York: Holt, Rinehart and Winston), 1-88.
Fodor, Jerry A. and Jerrold J. Katz
1964   *The structure of language, readings in the philosophy of language* (Englewood Cliffs, New Jersey: Prentice-Hall).
Franklin, Karl J.
9171   "Tagmemics and tagmemics rules", *Linguistics* 70: 25-44.
Fries, Peter H.
1970   "On pernicious recursion', *Wisconsin Papers in Linguistics* 1: 1-21.
Grimes, Joseph E.
to appear   *The thread of discourse.*
Hale, Austin
1972   "Syntactic matrices, an approach to descriptive comparability", to appear in *The Proceedings of the XIth International Congress of Linguists* (The Hague: Mouton), 259-271.
1973a   "Toward the systematization of display grammar", *Clause, Sentence, and Discourse Patterns in Selected Languages of Nepal,* Part I: General Approach, ed. by Austin Hale (Summer Institute of Linguistics Publications in Linguistics and Related Fields, Publication No. 40) (Norman: The Summer Institute of Linguistics), 1-37.
1974   "On the systematization of Box 4", *Advances in tagmemics,* ed. by Ruth M. Brend (Amsterdam: North-Holland),
Hale, Austin - David Watters
1973   "A survey of clause patterns", *Clause, sentence, and discourse patterns in selected languages of Nepal,* Part II: Clause, ed. by Austin Hale and David Watters (Summer Institute of Linguistics Publications in Linguistics and Related Fields, Publication No. 40) (Norman: Summer Institute of Linguistics), 175-249.
Hale, Austin - Thakurlal Manandhar
1973   "Case and role in Newari", *Nepal studies in Linguistics I* (Kirtipur: Summer Institute of Linguistics, Institute of Nepal and Asian Studies, Tribhuvan University), 39-54.
Harris, Zellig S.
1951   *Methods in structural linguistics* (Chicago: The university of Chicago Press).
Jacobs, Kenneth and Robert E. Longacre
1967   "Patterns and rules in Tzotzil grammar", *Foundations of Language* 3: 325-389.

88

Klammer, Thomas Paul
1971   *The structure of dialogue paragraphs in written English dramatic and narrative discourse* PhD dissertation, univ. of Michigan.
Lees, Robert B.
1964   Review of *String analysis of sentence structure* by Zellig S. Harris, *International Journal of American Linguistics* 30: 415-420.
Longacre, Robert E.
1960   "String constituent analysis", *Language* 36: 63-88.
1964a   *Grammar discovery procedures, a field manual* (= *Janua Linguarum*, series minor, 33) (The Hague: Mouton).
1964b   "Prolegomena to lexical structure", *Linguistics* 5: 5-24
1965a   "Some fundamental insights of tagmemics", *Language* 41: 65-76.
1965b   "Transformational parameters in tagmemic field structures", (*Monograph Series on Languages and Linguistics*, No. 18) (= *Report of the Sixteenth Annual Round Table Meeting on Linguistics and Language Studies*) (Washington, D.C.: Georgetown University Press) 43-58.
1968   *Discourse, paragraph and sentence structure in selected Philippine languages* (Summer Institute of Linguistics Publications in Linguistics and Related Fields, Publication No. 21) (Santa Ana: The Summer Institute of Linguistics).
1970a   "Sentence structure as a statement calculus", *Language* 46, 783-815.
1970b   "Hierarchy in language", *Method and theory in linguistics,* ed. by Paul L. Garvin (The Hague: Mouton), 173-195.
1972   *Hierarchy and universality of discourse constituents*: Discussion (Washington, D.C.: Georgetown University Press).
1973   "Hierarchy on the contemporary linguistic scene", *S.I.L. Papers on Semantics and Discourse*, ed. by Calvin R. Rensch (Unpublished lithographed collection, Summer Institute of Linguistics).
To appear "A hierarchical look at the English verb phrase", *Journal of Philippine Linguistics.*
Merrifield, William R.
1967   "On the form of rules in a generative grammar", (*Monograph Series on Languages and Linguistics* No. 20) (= *Report of the Eighteenth Annual Round Table Meeting on Linguistics and Language Studies*) (Washington, D.C.: Georgetown University Press), 43-55.
Pike, Kenneth L.
1948   *Tone languages* (Ann Arbor: University of Michigan Press).
1954   *Language in relation to a unified theory of the structure of human behavior*, Part I, preliminary edition (Glendale: Summer Institute of Linguistics).
1964a   "Discourse analysis and tagmeme matrices", *Oceanic Linguistics* 3, 5-25.
1964b   "Beyond the sentence", *College composition and communication* 15, 129-135. (Reprinted in Brend, 1972)
1964c   "A linguistic contribution to the teaching of composition", *College Composition and Communication* 15, 82-88.
1967a   *Language in relation to a unified theory of the structure of human behavior*, revised edition (The Hague: Mouton).
1967b   "Suprasegmentals in reference to phonemes of item, of process, and relation", *To honor Roman Jakobson. Essays on the occasion of his seventieth birthday* (The Hague: Mouton), 1545-1554.
1970   *Tagmemic and matrix linguistics applied to selected African languages* (Summer Institute of Linguistics Publications in Linguistics and Related Fields, Publication No. 23) (Norman: Summer Institute of Linguistics).
1971   "Crucial questions in the development of tagmemics – The Sixties and

Seventies ", (*Monograph Series on Languages and Linguistics* No. 24) (= *Report of the Twenty-Second Annual Round Table Meeting on Linguistics and Language Studies*) (Washington, D.C.: Georgetown University Press), 79-98.

1973a   "Sociolinguistic evaluation of alternative mathematical models: English Pronouns", *Language* 49: 121-160.

1973b   "Science fiction as a test of axioms concerning human behavior", *Parma Eldalamberon* 1:3.

Pike, Kenneth L. - Evelyn G. Pike

1973   *Grammatical analysis*, experimental draft (Santa Ana: Summer Institute of Linguistics).

1974   "Rules as components of tagmemes in the English verb phrase", *Advances in Tagmemics*, ed. by Ruth M. Brend (Amsterdam: North-Holland), 175-204.

Platt, John T.

1971   *Grammatical form and grammatical meaning, A tagmemic view of Fillmore's deep structure case concepts* (= North-Holland Linguistic Series No. 5) (Amsterdam: North-Holland).

Postal, Paul M.

1964   *Constituent structure: A study of contemporary models of syntactic description* (= Publication 30 of the Indiana University Research Center in Anthropology, Folklore, and Linguistics) (*International Journal of American Linguistics* 30.1, Part III).

1966   "Review of *Grammar discovery procedures* by Robert E. Longacre," *International Journal of American Linguistics* 32: 93-98.

Taylor, Doreen

1973   "Clause patterns in Tamang", *Clause, sentence, and discrouse patterns in selected languages of Nepal*, Part II: Clause, ed. by Austin Hale and David Watters (Summer Institute of Linguistics Publications in Linguistics and Related Fields, Publication No. 40) (Norman: Summer Institute of Linguistics), 81-174.

Watters, David E.

1973   "Clause patterns in Kham", *Clause, sentence and discourse patterns in selected languages of Nepal*, Part I, ed. by Austin Hale (Summer Institute of Linguistics Publications in Linguistics and Related Fields, Publication No. 40) (Norman: Summer Institute of Linguistics), 39-202.

Wise, Mary Ruth

1968   *Identification of participants in discourse: A study of aspects of form and meaning in Nomatsiguenga*. Ph. D. dissertation, The University of Michigan (= Summer Institute of Linguistics Publications in Linguistics and Related Fields, Publication No. 28[1971] (Norman: Summer Institute of Linguistics).

TOWARD THE DEVELOPMENT OF TAGMEMIC POSTULATES

KENNETH L. PIKE

University of Michigan and Summer Institute of Linguistics

The purpose of this paper is first to list certain concepts crucial to tagmemic theory; second, to indicate something of the time at which they first coalesced into a single coherent frame of reference (or were brought into sharper focus or, at a later date, added); and third, to give a set of preliminary postulates to indicate how one might try to indicate some of the logical connections between them.

I. A LIST OF SOME TAGMEMIC CONCEPTS

A. *Preliminary, generalized concepts:*

1. The observer standpoint is relevant to finding data; no 'thing-in-itself' (i.e. apart from an observer) is discussed by the theory.
   (a) Hence there are (phon)etic and (phon)emic views of a system, leading to outsider versus insider action toward perceived units of a system;
   (b) and static, dynamic and relational approaches may be taken toward the same body of data.
2. Analogy is perceivable by the native speaker. Hence slot and class enter the theory (when pairs of positions in a structure are filled by pairs of substitutable parts retaining the same perceived ratio between them).
3. Indeterminacy must be accepted as part of the data of actual behavior systems — not as a mere artifact of the analytical approach via a set of conceptual tools.
   (a) Hence, some change can be seen as occurring over bridges of indeterminacy;
   (b) and action at a distance is avoided.
4. Language is just one variety of behavior.
   (a) Hence language may be embedded in larger behavioral units;
   (b) a class of fillers of a slot may contain both verbal and non-verbal elements;

(c) and the most basic components of tagmemic theory are not language specific, but are rather generalizations which simultaneously cover both verbal and non-verbal purposive behavior.

B. *Specific working concepts*

We now give, in list form, twelve concepts which I explicitly use in explanations of tagmemics. I do not know how to eliminate any one of them and yet retain man as man, or language as we know it. In spite of their demonstrated heuristic value, the principles are so sufficiently general that I do not know how to test them by ordinary methods. Rather, I have suggested (1973) that if a science-fiction story could be written so that any one of the concepts could be eliminated, both explicity and implicitly, both from the imagined world and from the narrator's presuppositional framework, then it should be eliminated from the set claimed to be universal to human nature.So far neither I nor any of my colleagues or students has succeeded — although there have been one or more attempts.

1. There are emic units (or constituents) in every purposeful human system of behavior.
    (a) For these to be identifiable, contrastive features of the units must be found;
    (b) the range of variability of the unit must be in part specified, and must include some physical component (which might be neuro-logical, for units of thought); the variants might be free or conditioned, simple or complex;
    (c) The unit must be appropriate, in its occurrence, to a slot in some larger structure; it must be a member of an appropriate, analogous distributional class, in an appropriate sequence (or spacial array), and in a system (i.e. in a cell of a matrix with intersecting rows and columns of features relevant to that behavior).

2. Human behavioral units are hierarchically ordered, with smaller ones embedded in larger ones.
    (a) A hierarchy of purposive or meaningful units (lexemic ones for language) with some kind of cognitive features as part of their definitions will cover successively including units;
    (b) a physical hierarchy, as a kind of "carrier wave" for the other elements, will in language be made up of some combination of phonemes, syllables, stress groups, and still larger units up to

rhetorical periods;

(c) and an arrangement hierarchy, a grammatical one, will cover the successive inclusion of structures within the larger structures; with the tagmeme, which gives its name to the theory (as a composite of arrangement of slot-in-a-larger-unit, plus its filler class, plus its situational role, plus its semantic sub-category of the filler class) occurring as a sequential member of an emic construction, which in turn is one filler of a higher-level tagmemic slot.

3. Purposeful behavioral context is relevant to all emic units, and "infects" them with its meaning (or purposefulness, usefulness, fruitfulness, impact).
   (a) Hence *all* units of the theory are in some sense meaningful (having behavioral impact), that is, are form-meaning composites;
   (b) within such contexts of behavior, elements "bump", overlap, anticipate one another, or merge, setting up the conditions of change; the change occurs only over such a bridge of shared features (temporarily or permanently) shared by two units;
   (c) and behavior is intuited, by its performers, as occurring in frames of reference which we call universe of discourse, which affect the meanings of units and thus appropriateness of occurrence.

4. Observer perspective can vary: choice of standpoint, choice of topic of conversation, choice of level of complexity under attention, choice of criteria or appropriateness, are part of human nature.
   (a) A static (particle) view leads to performer focus on units, objects, things, events as wholes;
   (b) a dynamic (wave) view leads to performer focus on change, progress, decay (with focus often achieved by placing a unit in a nuclear position of grammatical or phonological structure), whereas out-of-focus elements would usually be arranged so as to be presented as structurally marginal, while indeterminacies could appear as "troughs" between nuclear peaks, (occasionally as totally merged nuclei);
   (c) and a relational (field) view leads to performer focus on relations between elements, downplaying attention to the units as such.

If units were to be lost, no persons, trees, or songs could be recognized by native performers. If hierarchy were to be lost, performers could never intuit the relation of part to whole. It the relevance of context were to be lost, communication of meaning and purpose would disappear. We would cease to be human.

II. ON THE HISTORY OF TAGMEMIC THEORY

A. *Preliminary dream*

I date the start of tagmemics, as a general theory, to the period from February 1948 to June 1949. I felt bored at studying phonological problems (phonetics, phonemics, tone, intonation) after having concentrated on them for thirteen years, and decided to shift my attention to grammar. As I turn back now, a quarter of a century later, to my unpublished notes for the summer of 1948, I note three emphases at that early stage:

(1) I wanted to study 'the total productive possibilities within the language', showing this through charts and description, which would aid in speaking a language or translating into it. That is, 'to emphasize that the goal of this chart is the productive use of the language'. (This is related in some sense to the current term "creativity".)

(2) I was emphasizing the fact that *linguists can recognize proportion* (analogies) in a series of appropriate sets of ratios with form and meaning, '*provided* [data from] *obvious physical contexts*' (such as must be used to discover meanings in a monolingual approach) are at some stage available. From this I was developing the terms 'relationship', 'the total unit', 'positions' (which are not physical sequence only, but functional parts of the relationships), 'lists' (in these positions) and the like.

(3) I was also testing the possibility — soon rejected — of finding a mechanical discovery procedure for immediate constituents of a grammatical construction by studying the sequence of its elements. That is, within a known sequence a, b, and c, I was wondering if one could determine whether b clustered directly with a, or with c, or with neither, merely by studying their permitted distributions.

In that summer of 1948 William Wonderly joined me in testing these three suggestions. Both of us were well acquainted with the idea of analogy from Bloomfield (1933: 408) as in *piano*: *pianos* = *radio* : *x*.

Working together, however, it became apparent that our search for a mechanical discovery procedure for the immediate constituents was — in our view at least – permanently hopeless. We would seem to be making progress at setting up segmentation rules, only to find constituents where the results were counter-intuitive. For example, the difference between the structure inside of words versus structure within phrases did not seem to be accounted for in our mechanical attempt. By the end of the summer, therefore, we abandoned the mechanical goal. The collapse of this attempt was not surprising to me, since I had already tried and abandoned a related approach for phonemics. In 1942 I had attempted a mechanical discovery procedure for studying allophonic distribution and had given it up. Instead, in the first (mimeographed) form of my *Phonemics* ([1943] 1947) I had replaced such a search procedure with a hypothesis-and-test approach (later called 'guess-and-check') by Longacre 1964: 11).

As a result of this double experience, by the fall of 1948 and spring of 1949 I was concentrating on the first two of the initial grammatical quests mentioned above, with the third abandoned.

B. *Breakthrough*

Early in 1949, however, I focused on a slightly different question: Would it be possible to find a useful bit of grammar which could be treated in a fashion analogous to the phoneme? If so, would it have descriptive properties related to the phoneme? The phoneme had been a practical element of alphabet formation for hundreds of years, but had been invisible to the eye of that type of scientist who is interested in mechanical detail ("accurate phonetics") rather than being interested in an element as a relational point in a composite system of form and meaning. If a comparable grammatical unit could be found, therefore, I expected that it would have been known – in some sense – to practical language teachers for a long time, but have some form-meaning composite characteristics which had made it difficult for the current generation of language scientists to recognize as relevant to their frame of reference. I called this not-yet-discovered unit a 'grameme' (later changed to 'tagmeme', Pike 1958, under the insistence of other linguists).

I started a generalized search through all kinds of grammar material known to me, focusing sometimes on formal elements, sometimes on semantic ones, and ranging from lexicon, to intonation, to constructions. At first nothing seemed to be useful, Then two concepts came together:

(a) The first was a functional position (or slot) with a list (or class) of elements occurring in that position, in a proportion such as *the*: *boy* = *a* : *boy* in which the ratio of determiner to the element it modifies is retained on both sides of the equation. This element was salvaged from the work of the previous summer, in which it was clear that the functional "meaning" of a pair of substituted forms could be recognized as invariant even when the break between immediate constituents was in doubt.

(b) The second was the concept that an element in a slot could be *a unit* even when that element was not analyzable into two grammatical parts. This material grew out of my earlier work (1944: 128, fn 8) where I abandoned the view (which seemed to me to be implicit in some approaches current at the time) that in order to be a grammatical unit an element must be made up of immediate (grammatical) constituents; and I replaced it with the view that in order to be a unit a grammatical element must fill a functional position in a construction. The difference in this decision had far-reaching consequences. Instead of searching first for immediate constituents, one searched rather for the relation of the element to something higher in the grammatical hierarchy. This required that hierarchy be an explicit component of the theory, and that one not attempt to analyze any unit strictly in terms of its internal structure, but rather that one must also look at a unit's relation to its including structures (i.e. its larger structural environment).

Thus unit in a slot of a ratio became crucial; and this suggested that I was getting close to the kind of element I was looking for. It emphasized unity; it emphasized distribution; and it seemed to hold out the possibility of having other characteristics which could interest me.

In order to try to get some idea as to how close I was coming to my preliminary goal, I decided (still in the spring of 1949) to try to compare these features with those of the classical phoneme. To aid in this comparison I attempted to condense the contents of classical phonemics into the smallest possible scope. I decided that I could summarize almost everything about the phoneme in terms of its contrast with other phonemes, in terms of its range of variability, and in terms of its distribution. Variability, in turn, had to be subdivided into free and conditioned types, and the conditioned variants into various sub-types. Here, then, I started checking to see if the same things could be said of the new proposed tagmeme. It seemed to me clear that the answer was yes. The subject tagmeme contrasted with the predicate tagmeme in its formal components and in its slot meaning. The subject tagmeme had a range of variability, in terms of the occurrence of specific members of the list which carry that function — as *big John* differed from *little John* subtagmemically. And the distribution of these elements was relevant to the including structure just as consonants and vowels were relevantly distributed within syllables.

From there, I checked to see if morphemes could be handled in the same way — and was satisfied that this proved true. Then I jumped to the generalized definition of any linguistic unit as an element which had contrast, range of variability, and significant distributional constraints. But in order to include the sentence in this definition, it was necessary to have something larger than the sentence — and eventually in order to keep a language as a unit, that language had to be treated as being distributed within a culture. It was at this point that the theory moved beyond linguistics proper, and included a cultural-behavioral setting as an essential component.

C. Early development

Up to this point, however, I was dealing with the generalized view of hierarchy current in the discipline at that time, that phonemes combine to make morphemes, morphemes combine to make words, words combine to make syntactic structures (cf. Trager 1949). I, also, had been deeply committed (as my linguistic diary of that semester recalls to my mind) to a hierarchical view of structure. Several years earlier (1943b) I had published on the hierarchical pyramiding of immediate constituents.

But soon I got a shock: I was attempting to analyze a written business letter, which in terms of the then climate in the USA would have been outside of the theory of linguistics proper, which was assumed to deal centrally only with oral matters. And there I noticed that I could differentiate a hierarchy of orthographic materials even before I knew any meaning — i.e. even for a language strange to me. Thus, I had a hierarchy of mechanical bits, analogous to a phonetic hierarchy, which could not be fitted in to the hierarchical scheme of phoneme-to-morpheme-to-syntax-to-meaning. In other words, the old hierarchy was inadequate to cover such data.

This forced a radical change in my thinking. I brought the syllable and stress group directly into a phonological hierarchy semi-independent of the grammatical one. It was not that I had ignored the syllable before — I had dealt with it substantially (1943a: 116); rather it was that a place for it in general theory was now added.

This in turn forced a new look at the rest of the system. If the phonological component had to be treated as incorporated into a hierarchy, it seemed to follow that the lexical one would have to be so also (with a morpheme at the base and a discourse or — say — a poem at the top). Similarly, the tagmemic hierarchy (of slots within slots, plus their respective fillers) would be expected to be hierarchically structured. In addition, the fact that this tagmemically-structured business letter was not oral, but written, led to the inclusion of all behavioral structures within the same

98

frame of reference (since it was soon clear that the slot-and-filler concept was in principle equally applicable not only to the written materials but also to all other nonverbal purposive human actions). The total of behavioral actions was obviously more extensive than the purely vocal ones, so this forced local material to be viewed within the context of nonverbal material, and the theory as a whole to refer to the total entity of human behavior. Since, however, the theory dealt only with elements which contained both form and meaning (and meaning has as its analog purpose or usefulness), nonpurposeful acts were excluded from its immediate purview.

Three other elements were important to the development of the theory in the first volumes, but took a less prominent place than those concerning units, as such, which provided the basic organizational framework. The first of these concerned indeterminacy and fusion (which I mentioned above); a second concerned grammatical case; and a third treated a phonemic chart as part of the theory.

Long before working on tagmemics proper, I had found it necessary, in an empirical view, to treat segments of sound – phones – as having determinate centers, but indeterminate borders. A segment was defined (1943a : 107) as 'a sound (or lack of sound) having indefinite borders but with a center that is produced by a crest or trough of stricture during the even motion or pressure of an initiator'. Other scholars of the time were more inclined to try to assume that a segment was determinate, and define the phone in reference to its borders. I avoided this deliberately since the borders were in fact empirically often not detectable by ear or by instruments. Thus the 1967b [1955] volume (Secs. 8.446, 8.51) gave schematic wave diagrams hierarchically ordered to show fusion and inclusion of phonemes within syllables. The tagmemic approach to indeterminacy in borders between sounds, and borders between morphemes, developed some years later into an explicit statement of grammar as wave (1967a) in which I demonstrated, on the basis of African data, that fusion between clauses (like the fusion between phonological units) could result in a re-alignment of the materials. A clause can become an auxiliary phrase, and the two enter into a hierarchy with wave-like characteristics. This appears to me to be one of the important elements of the theory which still needs extensive development.

As for the second, I had utilized the functional meaning of a position or slot as one of the features of the tagmeme. This component was used to distinguish (1967b [1954] 196) the tagmeme subject-as-actor from the tagmeme subject-as-goal; comparable contrastive relations between noun sequences within noun, noun-phrases were also indicated as important (1967b [1960]:458).

Third, a phonetic chart was treated as a significant element of the theory

(1967b [1955] 328-31) rather than being left as a mere heuristic display, helpful in getting started in understanding the nature of sounds or their components, relations or distinctive features.

D. The Sixties

Each of these elements became increasingly important to the theory, and were slowly developed after the completion of the initial volumes. Thus, treatment of grammatical meaning or role (that variety currently called *case* by many scholars when they discuss clauses) lay dormant for a decade until (in 1964b : 12) I attempted to make charts showing the criss-crossing of situational roles such as agent or goal, with grammatical slots such as subject or object. Matrices of these then opened the way to greater flexibility between the two systems (i.e. of grammatical arrangement and grammatical meaning). Major development of this area was undertaken by Becker (1967) just in time, before completion, to have reference also to work on case by Fillmore (1968). Forster (1964) had an important approach to structures which had dual internal arrangement related to case. Further work was done on case in the tagmemic framework by Cook (1970, 1971) and John Platt (1971 [1970]), with attention given to category-semantic features of tagmemes by Heidi Platt (1970). More recently, extensive illustrative material for four language families (Tibeto-Burman, Dravidian, Munda, Indo-European) has been given in Hale (1973) and in Trail (1973).

Similarly, the insistence that a phonetic chart become a relevant part of the theory was later brought to bear on grammar. By 1960 I was looking for a comparable matrix of elements of grammar, and moved into the handling of dimensional displays of clause structures (Pike: 1962 – where Larson provided the first example) and sentence structures. Still later, a group of articles brought the same concept to bear upon morphology, especially when morphemes in ancient fusion had led to lack of clearly segmented morpheme relations – as seen in New Guinea (Pike: 1963), North American Indian material (Pike and Erickson: 1964), and elsewhere.

In between the earlier, preliminary discussion of indeterminacies and matrix display and the more recent development of them, I had brought from physics the terms *particle, wave,* and *field* (1959) to illustrate for a nonlinguistic audience certain characteristics of units which could be seen either as static, or as dynamic, or as relational. Once adopted, this terminology proved so efficient in highlighting these language characteristics which I had been struggling with for a decade, that I continued to use it extensively. In addition to helping to label parts of the data it implied that the dynamic-static-relational perspectives should be maintained as parts of the theory, even though they were in some kind of uneasy balance, since it was not simple to join them logically in a single axiomatic approach. Here we chose to maintain the empirical data, reporting the facts of the possibility of multiple perspectives, rather than rejecting any one or two of them from the explicit theoretical framework in order to gain greater internal coherence.

In the sixties, in addition to developing the dynamic (wave) and relational (field) components, I gave further attention to high-level structures such as conversation, or poems (1964, and 1965) both as it concerns composition and poetic analysis (1971b). These conceptual tools, combined with the definition of unit in terms of contrast, variation, and distribution, allowed more explicit discussion of some characteristics of high level units – a description which had begun with a breakfast scene (1967b [1954] : Sec. 5.2.) a decade earlier. Longacre (e.g. 1964, 1968, 1972) has now contributed extensively in this area – as have Wise ([1968] 1971, with emphasis on participants), and Klammer (1971 with emphasis upon English dialog, while developing some of Longacre's concepts). We now make explicit a few places where changes came into the theory after the first volume (1954) and then we discuss certain unresolved problems or points where the theory is currently undergoing further change.

Longacre persuaded me that the 1967b [1954] volume was awkward in its requirement that the syntagmeme contain two obligatory elements. In the later dissertation by Pickett (1960) and in the Pike 1967b [1960] volume, therefore, the view was adopted that the syntagmeme did not have to have two obligatory constituents (although some syntagmemes did have two) but that it might have one obligatory, nuclear constituent with the construction expandable by the addition of an optional element. Therefore *the boy* and *John* can both be instances of noun phrases. The first would be a noun phrase with obligatory determiner; the second would be a personal noun phrase with a variant containing an optional modifier representing the same syntagmeme. This in turn forced the conclusion that there could be simultaneity of representations across more than one level by a single element – as *John* would be the head of the noun phrase while simultaneously representing the full phrase within the subject slot of *John came home*. In *Big John came home*, the morpheme *John* would be the head of the noun (compare *Johnny*) and of the noun phrase, but would not be the full filler of the subject slot. (For recent treatment of tagmemic constituents of the noun phrase see Fries, 1970). (This also allowed the term 'tagmeme' to function early but relativistically on all levels of the hierarchy.)

The implications of this emphasis are continuing to have a strong impact on materials not yet in print. In a recent treatment of the grammatical hierarchy, for example, Pike and Pike (mimeograph 1975, and see Huttar 1973) treat independent clause as a variety of sentence, in which amplifications of the sentence can be made by a further modifying clause. Thus *When John had finished eating, he came home*, would be a single grammatical sentence with two clauses, the second independent; but *John came home* would also be a sentence, which is simultaneously an independent clause in the conversational exchange: *What happened? ... John came home.* It is crucial, in the seventies, that this lesson not be forgotten in treating sentences; their potential distribution in slots, paragraphs or in dialog types must enter into their definitions; a mere listing of inner elements of form or of propositional content is in itself insufficient for our purposes.

A second change in the theory came from the impact of work by John Crawford (1963) about the same time (in time to be mentioned in the third volume of the text 1967b [1960]: 520 but not in time for the re-working of the theory for that volume). He suggested that the phonological hierarchy should be split into two subhierarchies – first into a hierarchy of phonemic segmental content, and secondly into a kind of phonological-slot hierarchy. He came out, therefore, with a phonological tagmeme paralleling the grammatical tagmeme, each with its fillers. If he were then to use units of the 1954 lexical hierarchy as a filler of the grammatical tagmeme, he would end up with a two-by-two dual hierarchical system, rather than the three simpler hierarchies which I had had. I continued to feel uncomfortable with this, thinking it did not meet some of our needs for three hierarchies, so continued to look for a way to use his two bifurcated hierarchies, while preserving a parallel third-lexemic one.

A third important change in tagmemic theory was brought in by Wise (1971 [1968]) in a attempt to solve this problem: She separated the old 1954 lexical hierarchy from a new lexemic one. Whereas the lexical hierarchy had been completely coterminous with specific morpheme sequences, her lexemic hierarchy did not have to be coterminous with the grammatical one or with the lexical items but was more directly related to elements in the events or elements of the environment. Thus, specifically, the lexemic structure of a narrative included as one of its features the chronological sequence – even when the story was told in an order which was not chronological. This factor is having increasing impact on my own current work, in searching for lexemic invariants in multiple tellings of the same story (see Pike and Pike 1972). On the other hand, her detailed treatment of the lexemic units has not yet been in general assimilated into theoretical and applied treatments of the theory.

In the postulates of this present article I attempt to preserve this suggestion (that lexemic hierarchy is not the lexical one) but differ by trying to keep case relations such as agent or undergoer as part of the grammatical tagmeme. Evelyn G. Pike has urged that the four-cell tagmeme of grammar be paralled with comparable four-celled tagmemes of phonology and lexemics. I here make tentative suggestions in that direction, for both. If the approach can be sustained, with appropriate modifications, then a further advance in theory will result in a different kind of balance in the treatment of hierarchies from those currently available. Previously Elson and Pickett (1960) had provided discussion and pedagogical drills for slot and class of the grammatical hierarchy (supplemented by drills by Merrifield and others 1960); our first attempt at the further pedagogical work gives drills in the four-celled grammatical tagmeme (slot, class, role, category) but does not provide drills needed to implement the lexemic four-celled suggestions being developed here.

A summary of the further specific developments of tagmemic theory in the decade of the sixties is given in Pike (1971a). Tagmemic bibliographies, annotated, are available in Pike (1966) and Brend (1970 and 1972). We might mention, specifically, however, that extension of the theory to touch upon other problems (such as music, in Chenowith and Bee, 1971) has been undertaken.

E. *The Seventies*

What could we expect for the remainder of the seventies? Presumably we will have more work on roles and categories of the grammatical hierarchy and attempts to clarify detail concerning the lexemic hierarchy, along with efforts to relate the theory of tagmemics to transformational-generative grammar, stratificational grammar, and other views. Further development of mathematical formulas should occur, following up the application of mathematical group theory to discourse structures (Pike and Lowe 1969, Poythress 1973, Bold 1972, Wise and Lowe 1972, and Pike 1973b). With the growing interest in sociolinguistics and psycholinguistics, it would seem that there should be further development in these areas since each, like tagmemics, has interests in behavior other than that of linguistic activity alone. From the tagmemic perspective, for example, the structuring of the speaker himself may be brought to bear as a determinant of the characteristics of a conversation (Bernstein and Pike, 1974).

In connection with conversation, paragraph and sentence structure there should be further handling of grammatical meanings, and perhaps a heuristically-useful etics of proposition types directly related to tagmemic analysis (cf. Trail: 1973 with relation to earlier work by John Beekman, Beekman and Callow, 1975, Larson, 1975 and others. See also Ballard,

Conrad and Longacre 1971.

An important change already underway in the concept of hierarchical structure includes an attempt to classify the levels of the grammatical hierarchy into pairs. Instead of a single progression of successive inclusion (from morpheme to word, phrase, clause, sentence, paragraph, monologue, dialogue, conversation) we are attempting to set up a paired level of the hierarchy itself as a form-meaning composite, but with such a paired level having simple forms and expanded forms (i.e. a pair of related levels), plus a shared semantic component. Thus, in Fig. 1 (taken from Pike and Pike 1973:32; and see also Huttar 1973)

Communication load (the meaning of the paired level)	Minimum unit	Unit potentially expanded from the minimum.
Social interaction	Exchange	Conversation
Theme Development	Paragraph	Monologue
Proposition	Clause	Sentence
Term	Word	Phrase
Lexical package	Morpheme	Morpheme cluster (sometimes, stem)

Figure 1
Chart of paired grammatical levels

both clause and sentence have 'proposition' (or "assertion") as meaning; but a minimum sentence of propositional type may be an independent clause; a minimum unit of social interaction is a verbal exchange (a dialogue with just one utterance and one response), which may be expanded into a conversation. These judgments, in turn, relate to the judgment mentioned above that a word under certain circumstances could be considered a minimum phrase.)

In addition to allowing us to have meaning more closely tied to hierarchy this paired-level approach has the advantage that a simple, minimum hierarchical structure in some one instance may be considered "complete" without the necessity of there being present every level of the total expanded hierarchy; and it opens the door for further degrees of expansion (e.g. via a clause cluster, a unit between clause and sentence), if this proves desirable.

Tench (1972) has suggested the development of a paired phonological hierarchy, following our grammatical one. In it the phoneme would be the minimum unit of the lowest level, with a phoneme cluster comprising the expanded unit of that level (e.g. *str* of *string*; or perhaps *ou* of *about*). The syllable would be the minimum unit and the rhythm group the expanded unit, in the next higher level. (Tench suggests as further possible pairs, tone [intonation] group [or stress group] with breath group; phonological paragraph with phonological discourse [monologue]; and phonological dialogue with phonological conversation.) His handling of the phoneme cluster encourages us to use morpheme clusters (instead of stems, only) in the grammatical hierarchy.

In form and meaning, in hierarchy and unit, in behavioral context and man-in-context, development must continue – and some of that development will surface in the writings of other authors in this present volume.

III. TENTATIVE POSTULATES FOR TAGMEMICS

Early in 1971 under prodding – with helpful suggestions – from Lowe and P. Fries, I attempted to try to show how some of these tagmemic concepts might be connected in postulational form. Specifically, they wanted to see the introduction of the terms particle, wave, and field delayed until after the introduction of other terms, rather than being used early in the description of the theory. On the other hand, Evelyn G. Pike, co-authoring with me a text on grammatical analysis, wanted early in the postulates the terms for proportion in order that the use of the terms slot and class, in early lessons in the heuristic text, could be justified. I give now the first, preliminary, attempt at such a postulational set leading toward the inclusion of concepts discussed in Section I.

There are ar least three gaps which future work needs to fill: (1) The postulates are not checked out for acceptable logical form and consistency, but are presented as a working paper for those who already wish access to them. (2) They do not go into enough detail to cover all known aspects of verbal structure; the treatment ends soon after the general behavioral concepts of Section I have been mentioned. (3) They start from one chosen point, whereas I feel strongly that I should like to see several alternative sets of postulates with alternative starting points (inasmuch I have already shown, 1973b, that alternate sets of formalisms characterizing "all and only" certain elements of behavior are not all equally useful for the kind of study of linguistic behavior which is interested in the contrastive pathways of behavior by which these same behavioral units can be arrived at).

A. *Check List of Terms in the Postulates*

Numerous terms such as 'person' and 'exist' are introduced into the postulates without definition in capital letters, and then serve as primitive elements in relation to which technical terms such as 'slot' or 'frame' are defined. Since some of these undefined terms might themselves be defined under an alternate set of postulates, and since I wish the reader to be aware of these crucial presuppositions insofar as I am aware of them myself, I give the undefined terms in italics. If my readers do not share my usage of these undefined terms, understanding between us may be interrupted, and a different starting point might be helpful for them. Since, further, I should like the crucial order of my introduction of terms to be seen by the reader as easily as possible, so that speculation as to alternative orders might be made easier for him, I first list in Section B the terms themselves listed (in caps or italics) only at their first occurrence, by postulate number. Then, in Section C, the postulates themselves will be given.

B. *The List of undefined and defined terms, in the order of their introduction*

1. PERSON, EXIST, OBSERVE, ITEM
    1a. *observer*
    1b. CAPABLE, PARTIALLY
2. PERFORM, ACT, CHANGE, SITUATION, PART
3. PERCEIVING RELATIONS
    3a. *role*
4. CLOSER, *neighborhood*
    4a. APPROPRIATELY, SAME *slot, frame*
    4b. SET, *substitution class, filler class, member*
    4d. *category*
5. PRECEDES, FOLLOWS, *ordering*
    5a. TIME, SPACE, *sequence*
    5b. BESIDE, BETWEEN, PHYSICAL, PHYCHOLOGICAL, *location*
    5c. *pattern*
6. *system*
    6a. *context*
    6b. *distribution*
    6d. PARTICIPANT, *native*, BROUGHT UP, FOREIGN
    6e. SHARE, COMPONENT
    6f. *proportion, analogous*
    6g. INITIATING, RESPONSE, ELICITATION

6i.   *encounter*

6ii.   *dialogue,*

6iii. *minimum dialogue, expanded dialogue, counter elicitation, complex or compound dialogue,* INCLUDED, *exchange*

6iv. DISCUSSION, *independent, dependent*

6v.   *independent sentence*

6vi. *word*

6vii. OPENER, GREETING, *opening initiator, opening response, closing initiator, closing response*

7.   INCLUDED, *hierarchy*

    7e. *form, constituent*

8.   ATTITUDE, impact, AFFECT, UNDERSTANDING, ELICIT, ATTEMPT, EXPRESS

    8a. *human behavior*

    8b. *relevant, meaning, purpose, usefulness, fruitfulness*

    8c. *form-meaning composite*

9.   ASSOCIATED, *universe of discourse*

    9a. ACADEMIC, *frame of reference*

    9b. *theory*

10. CAUSE, INTERACTION

11. *context-focused issue*

12. JUDGE

    12a. DIFFERENT

    12b. *variant*

    12c. REPEATED OCCURRENCES, DESCRIBED

    12d. *conditioned variant, free variant, systemically conditioned, style conditioned*

    12e. *independently different, consistently different*

13. *contrast*

    13a. *noncontrastive*

    13b. *contrastive feature*

    13c. *identificational feature*, RECOGNIZE

    13d. *paradigmatic, syntagmatic*

    13e. *syntagmatic*

14. *unit*

    14a. *well-described*

    14b. *emic unit, emic feature*

    14c. PRELIMINARY, *etic$_1$ unit, etic$_2$*

15. PHYSICAL

    15a. *phonological hierarchy*

    15b. *phoneme*

15c. *syllable*, PROMINENT, CENTRAL, INDEPENDENTLY-OCCURRING, *syllabic, nuclear, nonsyllabic,*
15d. *vowel, consonant, semi-consonant, semi-vowel*
15e. *rhythm group, stress group, pause group*
16 *morpheme*, MANIFESTED, REALIZED
17. *grammatical tagmeme*
   17a. *slot-as-role: class-as-category, cohesion*
   17b. *grammatical arrangement, grammatical situation, grammatical function, grammatical filler*
   17c. *grammatical construction, syntagmeme*
18. *level*
   18b. *minimal and expanded paired syntagmeme types, paired hierarchy, grammatical nucleus*
   18c. *phrase*, TERM, NAME
   18d. *independent clause*, PROPOSITION, ASSERTION
   18e. *paragraph, monologue*, THEME DEVELOPMENT, *exchange, conversation,* social interaction, MORPHEME CLUSTER, STEM, *lexical package*
   18g. OPTIONAL, OBLIGATORY, DISJUNCT, DEFINITION, CONJUNCT
19. *phonological paired hierarchy, segmental, phoneme, phoneme culster, syllable, rhythm unit, response slot*
20. *phonological tagmeme, phonological construction*
   20a. STRESS, RIME
21. FOCUS, TALK ABOUT, CULTURE, REAL, IMAGINARY
22. *paraphrase set*
   22a. *concept, referent*
   22c. SENSE (as meaning)
   22d. *lexeme*
   22e. *synonym*
   22f. *homophonous*
23. *lexical*, DICTIONARY
24. ENCYCLOPEDIA
25. *lexemic hierarchy, referential hierarchy*
   25b. *taxonomic classification*, SPECIFIC, GENERIC
26. *lexemic construction*
27. *lexemic tagmeme*
   27a. *lexemic arrangement slot, lexemic filler class, lexemic situational role, lexemic filler category*
29. INSTANCE
30. BORDER
32. *norm, co-terminous*

32a. *indeterminancy*
32b. *morphophonemically-different variants*
32c. *morphophonemically-different variants*
33. *analytical focus*
   33a. *primary secondary and tertiary focus, presupposition out of focus*
   33b. *discourse analysis, linguistic study of literature, morphology*
34. *system of levels*
   34a *particle view*
   34b. *static*
35. *dynamic perspective*
   35a. *simultaneous units, portmanteau*
   35b. *wave perspective*
   35c. DEGREE OF ARTICULATORY OPENESS
36. *relational (field) perspective*
   36a. *component-times-component matrix, feature matrix*
   37a. NETWORK
   37b. RULE
   37c. INVENTORY
   37d. *complementarity*
   37f. *scientist*

C. *The Postulates in Preliminary Form*

1. PERSONS EXIST, and OBSERVE ITEMS around them.
   1a. Perons are *observers*
   [The postulates begin by introducing John Doe as a person, an entity. The first postulate introduces such a person, observing, as more basic than the thing which he observes, insofar as the sequence of postulates is concerned.]
   1b. Persons are CAPABLE of observing items PARTIALLY known to them through these observations.
   [This brings in partial capability, rather than any assumed theoretial necessity for total observation.]
2. Persons PERFORM (or ACT), such that they themselves CHANGE, as does the SITUATION within which they perform and of which they (as performers), and their performances, and items are PARTS.
   2a. An observer can observe himself as part of the situation in which he is observing and acting.
3. Persons are capable of PERCEIVING RELATIONS between performances and situations, between performances and self, and between self and situation.

3a. When persons or items perform in relation to their environment, they may be said to have a *role* in relation to that situation.

4. An observer may perceive an item x as part of a situation; if the y-part of an environment is perceived to be CLOSER to x than to a z-part, the y-part is a *neighborhood* of x.

4a. If m and n are observed as APPROPRIATELY occurring in the SAME neighborhood, then the empty place where m, n, may occur is *slot*; a slot plus its neighborhood is a *frame*.

4b. Since the SET m, n, occur in the same frame, they may be called by the analyst observer a *substitution class*, or a *filler class*, and m, n are each *members* of that substitution class.

4c. Items in frames have a role relative to that frame.

4d. The class of items which can appropriately act in a particular role of a situation form a *category* of items, which is a subset of the filler class.

5. When the observer perceives that an item PRECEDES or FOLLOWS its neighborhood we may say that *ordering* has been perceived; similarly, when one item is perceived as being in relation to some other item, we say that a relation has been perceived.

5a. Ordering in relation to a preceding or following item in TIME or SPACE may be said to be part of a *sequence* in its neighborhood.

5b. Items perceived as being BESIDE, BETWEEN, or next to other items in space (whether PHYSICAL or PSYCHOLOGICAL) are seen in a given *location* in that relationship.

5c. When a number of items are perceived as ordered in some way, the abstracted relationship between them may be called a *pattern*.

6. When x and y enter into each other's definitions via their relationship to each other, the items plus the relationship comprise a *system*. [By this definition the system is not the sum of the items, nor the abstracted relationship, but the items-in-relationship.]

6a. The neighborhood of an item ordered in relation to a system will be called *context*.

6b. The sum of the appropriate neighborhoods of x ordered in a system is the *distribution* of x.

6c. Hence, the distribution of x refers to its occurrence, potentially but appropriately in class, location (or sequence), and system.

6d. A PARTICIPANT observer or actor is *native* to a system, when he has been BROUGHT UP in that system; otherwise the oberser of that system is FOREIGN to it. [So far, nothing has been said which is language specific-all of the postulates can apply to nonverbal behavior. This is supposed to hold true for all the basic postulates until language is specifically brought in.]

6e. Two items in a system may be related in various ways: e.g. (1) they may be neighbors in a sequence and SHARE a common COMPONENT, or (ii) they may both have locations in a system, as members of a distribution class.

6f. Given x preceding y in a system, and z preceding y in that system, if the relation between x and y is perceived by the observer as the same as that between z and y, then xy and zy are in *proportion* to one another; and x and z are *analogous* to one another.

6g. Action between two persons may be ordered in a system such that an INITIATING act by the one person may be appropriately followed by a RESPONSE act, by the second person, which fulfills the ELICITATION of the first act, positively or negatively.

6gi. Such a nonverbal sequence is an *encounter*.

6gii. A verbal sequence of this kind is a *dialogue*.

6giii. A *minimum dialogue* contains a verbal initiation (or elicitation) and response; an *expanded dialogue* may contain *counter elicitation* elements which do not fulfill the initiating elicitation, but replaces it with an elicitation by the second person of the first. A *complex* or *compound dialogue* may be made up of several minimum or expanded dialogues in sequence, by the same speakers, and each of the INCLUDED dialogues is a dialogue *exchange*.

6giv. The initiating part of the DISCUSSION in a dialogue is called *independent*. If the response part is not able to serve appropriately also as initiating part, it is called *dependent*.

6gv. The minimum independent initiating part of a dialogue is an *independent sentence*.

6gvi. The minimum dependent (response) part of a dialogue is a *word*.

[Thus words may be members of the distribution class filling a response slot. But only sentences er sequences of sentences may be members of the distribution class of independent initiating sentences.]

6gvii. Before the discussion proper, a dialogue may be begun with an OPENER (or GREETING) slot and its fillers, with *opening initiator* and *opening* response. Similarly, there may be *closing initiators* and *closing responses*.

[None of these are under the constraints of the discussion

initiators and discussion responses of 6giv-vi.]
7. A set of successively INCLUDED items comprises a *hierarchy* of items.
7a. Hierarchical relationship is one kind of ordering.
7b. An item of a hierarchy occurring in a neighborhood may itself be made up of a smaller neighborhood plus an INCLUDED item:
7c. Items in a hierarchy are distributed within the hierarchy.
7d. Items in a hierarchy are systemically related via that hierarchy.
7e. Any items which are a part of the hierarchical system of substitution classes are *forms* or *constituents* of that system.
8. Within a system of human acts (and the holding of ATTITUDES viewed as act, forms are said to have an *impact*, if native or foreign observers see that they sometimes AFFECT that action, or if they affect the UNDERSTANDING of those acting, or if they ELICIT or ATTEMPT to elicit acts or understanding of acts or situations, or if they EXPRESS or attempt to express attitudes towards acts or situations.
8a. Human acts may be called *human behavior*.
8b. Forms having such impact are *relevant* to the system, or may be said to have *meaning* (or *purpose, usefulness, fruitfulness*).
8c. Forms in conjunction with their area of relevance are *form-meaning composites*.
9. A set of meanings, tacitly or explicitly in a system, along with its ASSOCIATED set of form-meaning composites and contexts will be called a *universe of discourse*.
9a. A universe of discourse identified for purposes of serving as background accepted for certain ACADEMIC discussions may be called a *frame of reference*.
9b. A frame of reference used to help one understand the relationship between some elements of a given situation or set of situations will be called a *theory*.
9c. An extended discussion may develop its own universe of discourse.
9d. Universes of discourse can be hierarchically ordered, or occur in a system of universes of discourses.
10. Item x can affect item y (i.e. item x can CAUSE y to change) only if x shares with y membership in a system; and items x and y will at the moment of INTERACTION be neighbors in that system.
[That is, we are allowing no action at a distance, in some sense.]
10a. Change which has been caused in one item by another will be seen or described relative to its place in some universe of discourse, where the two are for the moment, at least, neighbors.
[That is, the neighbors must be related in some kind of a larger

unified frame of reference, no matter how diverse they be, if they are to interact.]

11. When as a technical observer I am giving prime attention to features of a form-meaning composite (or to the association of sets of form-meaning composites) within a universe of discourse, I shall speak of *context-focused issues*.
[In 6a specific context was in view; here the more abstract nature of context in relation to the theory as a whole is given.]

12. A native or foreign observer can sometimes JUDGE (rightly or wrongly) that a certain form-meaning composite from a universe of discourse is in some sense the same composite, but has been changed because of interaction with its neighbors in that universe of discourse. [By using form-meaning composite we are moving away from random items toward emic unit. By using universe of discourse we leave out some irrelevancies but leave the door open to style conditioning. By using both native and foreign observers we leave technical analysis as a special variety of native behavior under certain conditions.]

   12a. Such occurrences relative to the composite as a whole (including all of its repetitions) are said to be DIFFERENT by (native or foreign) analysts.

   12b. When repetitions of a form-meaning composite are observed as different items x and y, they are called *variants* of that composite.

   12c. When a form-meaning composite is judged to change during REPEATED OCCURRENCES of that composite, it may be DESCRIBED in reference to a selection of a set of two or more items x and y in its various locations.

   12d. When an observer judges a variant of a form-meaning composite to have been caused by interaction with its neighborhood it may be called a *conditioned variant*; if change in the composite is observed without that change being judged as caused by the neighborhood it may be called a *free variant*; if the change is judged to be caused by occurrence of the composite in a particular system, or style, the variant may be called *systemically conditioned*, or *style conditioned*.

   12e. Items which are different but which are non-conditioned are *independently different*; items which are different but which are not freely different are *consistently different*.

13. If items x and y within a system are judged to be different, and to be relevant to the difference between form-meaning composites of that system, and if they are neither conditioned variants nor free variants

then x is said to *contrast* with y.

13a. Items which are independently, consistently different are in contrast. Other items are *non-contrastive*.
[This phrasing is added, since it is the most convenient one I have found for pedagogical purposes.]

13b. Parts or components or x which lead the observer to judge that x is in contrast with y are *contrastive features* of x.

13c. Contrastive features of a form-meaning composite may serve the observer as *identificational features,* allowing him to RECOG-NIZE that composite.

13d. When items x and y contrast as members of a substitution class, the contrast is *paradigmatic*.

13e. When items x and y are respectively members of different filler classes which are used to define hierarchical locations for distributional statements of other items, they are in *syntagmatic* contrast.
[For example, the sound /i/ and the sound /y/ in English are members of vowel and consonant classes, respectively, which are used to help define locations in the syllable — which in turn becomes a matrix for more complex distributional statements.]

14. A form-meaning composite of a system within a universe of discourse, with or without observed variants but in contrast with other composites of that system, is a *unit*.
[Item is not equivalent to unit.],

14a. A unit is *well-defined* when there have been specified its contrastive-identificational features, its variants, and its distribution in class, sequence, or other location and in a system of a universe of discourse.
[We are now approaching the goal of reaching emic unit via the path from observer through neighborhood, form-meaning composite, and change.]

14b. A unit meeting these specifications in the judgment of the analyst, native or foreign, may be called an *emic unit*; and contrastive features of an emic unit may be called *emic features*.

14c. When the foreign analyst (or the native speaker acting as an analyst) gives PRELIMINARY or tentative judgment as to the emic character of an item or of a feature, this is treated as an $etic_1$ unit or feature. If the analyst judges his work to be finished but finds that non-contrastive free or conditoned variants or features are left in his description, these variants or features are also said to be $etic_2$ (but indexed to show the different kind of

114

judgment involved).
[Unit, in our most abstract terms, is now finished. We still need to differentiate types of units via the kinds of hierarchy which they enter, and via the levels of each hierarchy.]

15. The PHYSICAL units comprising or included in form-meaning composites may themselves form part of a physical hierarchy.

15a. In language this physical hierarchy is called the *phonological hierarchy*.

15b. The minimum emic segment of the phonological hierarchy is called a *phoneme*.

15c. The immediate distributional unit for describing the occurrence of these phoneme segments and their relations is the *syllable*, in which the most PROMINENT or CENTRAL or INDEPENDENTLY-OCCURRING segment (or segment sequence) is *syllabic* and *nuclear*; the non-nuclear elements are *non-syllabic*.

15d. Phoneme types which in a particular language are consistently syllabic are *vowels* of that language; if consistently non-syllabic they are *consonants*; segments with an intermediate distributional role may be called *semi-consonants* or *semi-vowels*.

15e. The immediate distributional unit for descriptive occurrence of syllables is the *rhythm group* (or *stress group*), with a stressed syllable (or syllable cluster) as nuclear, and nonstressed syllables as marginal. The included distributional unit for the stress group is the *pause group*. The pause group, in turn, is embedded in higher distributional units, and so on.

16. Units which are minimum form-meaning composites carrying characteristically but not exclusively meanings of a "distionary" type (names, actions, quantities, relations) are called *morphemes*. and are distributed as members of a filler class in the grammatical hierarchy. They are MANIFESTED (or REALIZED) by units (or components of units) of the phonological hierarchy.

17. The combination of (i) a slot in a grammatical frame, in conjunction (ii) with its situational role and (iii) its abstracted substitution class of emic lexical units x, z, and (iv) its category, is a *grammatical tagmeme* with its four tagmemic features.

17a. These four grammatical features may be given a notation: *slot-as-role: class-as-category* (or *cohesion* instead of category).

17b. In an alternate notation the tagmemic features may be classified as *grammatical arrangement* (made up of the slot position and the filler class of morphemes or morpheme sequences) or as *grammatical situation* (made up of the functional role, and the

	Function	Filler
Arrangement	Slot	Class
Situation	Role	Category

Figure 2
Grammatical four-cell tagmemic display

functional category subdividing the filler class); intersecting with *grammatical function* (slot and role) and *grammatical filler* (class and category). See Fig. 2.

18. Emic grammatical constructions may be displayed as entering a hierarchy which may be characterized as a system of successively inclusive kinds of construction types, or *levels*.

18a. Certain pairs of grammatical levels have a particular kind of behavioral impact (i.e., meaning);

18b. The members of a pair of levels may be related as *minimum* to *expanded paired syntagmeme types*, in which a minimum unit may serve as *grammatical nucleus* for the expanded unit; these pairs of levels compirse a *paired hierarchy*.

[The term minimum is used relative to the kind of construction in view. It may be used to refer to a particular emic construction and its expansion without change of emic level (as *He came home* and *He came home yesterday* are both on the clause level); but it may also be used relative to the paired members of a level of the hierarchy (as *He drives the car a great deal* is simultaneously a clause and a sentence, but *He drives the car a great deal since he has a lot of money tied up in it* is an expanded sentence that is not a single clause).

18c. Thus, a word syntagmeme may be expanded to a *phrase* syntagmeme. Both word and phrase carry the meaning of TERM (or NAME).

[Compare *John* and *big John*.]

18d. Similarly, an *independent clause* serves as a nucleus of most sentence types; the pair share the meaning of PROPOSITION (or ASSERTION).

18e. The hierarchical pair composed of *paragraph* and *monologue* have the meaning of THEME DEVELOPMENT; the pair including *exchange* and *conversation* has the meaning of SOCIAL INTERACTION; the pair with morpheme and stem or, perhaps

better, MORPHEME CLUSTER (or, sometimes, STEM) has the
meaning of *lexical package*.

18f. Any one language may have an emic system of emic levels which
includes all of the etic ones listed; or it may omit some, or
combine some, or add other levels not suggested here.
[If it turns out that further levels need to be added for some
languages, then this generalized etic scheme will need to be
amplified (e.g. by the addition of a level for an emic clause
cluster; or by the addition of a level for literature say, in the form
of a level for section or chapter; or a level for a coordinate stem
or clause of sentence.]

18g. If, within a construction, xy may occur independently of y (but
not vice versa) in a slot which also may be filled by xy as a whole,
then x is nuclear or central to the construction but y is both
marginal and OPTIONAL. Likewise, x is nuclear and y is marginal
even if both x and y are OBLIGATORY, provided that x as a unit
has approximately the same meaning as does xy. Other conditions,
not listed here, may also specify nuclearity (that is, by a
DISJUNCT DEFINITION, not a CONJUNCT one.)
[So, also, for example, sentences and various other emic units
need disjunct definitions (Cf. C. Fries 1952: 60-61, with
disjunct definition of a baseball "strike".]

19. An etic *phonological paired hierarchy*, paralleling our the grammatical one,
may also be used for phonology, (Tench) with *segmental
phoneme* and *phoneme cluster* as minimum and expandable segmental
phonological lowest level; the *syllable* and *rhythm group* as the next
level; the syllable is the minimum normal pronounceable filler of an
utterance or the *response slot*.

20. Phonological units, like grammatical ones, may be related via a four-cell
matrix representing a *phonological tagmeme*. Phonological tagmemes in
emic relationship comprise *phonological constructions*.

20a. In the arrangement row, function would be seen as a slot in a
larger unit (e.g. the stress slot in a STRESS group), whereas class
would be the type of pattern of sequence of units (e.g. a CVC
syllable pattern).

20b. In the situational row, function would be seen as a role in some
generalized pattern of the particular discourse (e.g. as stressed
role in iambic pentameter), whereas the class would be a
discourse-conditioned subset of the more inclusive pattern (e.g. a
RIMING pair of CVC such as *-ove* of *love* and *dove*).

21. Performers can FOCUS on, and TALK ABOUT items or situations

	Function	Class
System arrangement:	e.g. end position in a poetic line	e.g. CVC
Discourse situation:	e.g. rime	e.g. *-ove*

Figure 3
Phonological tagmeme

which they (or their CULTURE) select for attention from some physical
or nonphysical, REAL or IMAGINARY, situation.

21a. The items or situations focused on and talked about can be given
a name in the form of a term, or a lexical package.

21b. When the performer talks about an item or situation, he may do
so by using proposition and theme development to relate that
item or situation to other items or situations or to parts of items
or situations.

22. The performer may use a *paraphrase set* of morphemes or morpheme
sequences to talk about the same item or situation in different ways in
a discourse, by using different morphemes or morphemes sequences
which substitute for the first-appearing member of the set in that
discourse.

22a. Members of a paraphrase set share a meaning which may be called
a *concept*; the item named by the paraphrase set is its *referent*.

22b. A morpheme or morpheme sequence may have several meanings
differing according to the universe of discourse or situation in
which it is said.

22c. A concept may be one of the SENSES (meanings) of a complex
of meanings of a morpheme or a morpheme sequence.
[Such as a dictionary entry might give as part of a list for a
morpheme or morpheme sequence.]

22d. A concept plus some one member of its paraphrase set is a
lexeme.

22e. Two lexiemes from the same paraphrase set are
synonyms relative to that universe of discourse.
[Synonyms are not, therefore, treated directly in relation to
dictionary items.]

22f. When a member of one paraphrase set is manifested by the same
morpheme or morpheme set as is a member of another paraphrase
set, the joint manifestations are *homophonous*.

118

[By this, two senses of a single morpheme lead to homonymity of the occurrences of that morpheme in different universes of discourse.]

23. A morpheme or unitary morpheme sequence is a *lexical* unit; and a small lexical unit) – say of word length – with its various senses comprises a DICTIONARY entry.

24. A lexeme (or unitary complex of lexemes) comprises an entry in an ENCYCLOPEDIA.
    [The term *pope* would be a dictionary entry; *Pope John XXIII* would be an encyclopedic one.]

25. A *lexemic hierarchy* occurs, with lexemes as its minimal units.
    [Just as morphemes are minimal units in the grammatical-construction hierarchy.] (Elsewhere we may call lexemic *referential*.)
    25a. The conceptual relation of part to whole is a feature of the lexemic hierarchy.
        [Thus, 'term' and 'proposition' are themselves concepts with the terms as parts of the propositions, and with the terms related to each other by the proposition. See 28e, below.]
    25b. A *taxonomic classification* has successive class inclusion of units from SPECIFIC to GENERIC, with every member of each level of the classification being an instance of every higher level of that classification.
        [But this is not true of the part-whole lexemic hierarchy.]

26. A *lexemic construction* is a conceptual item viewed as a whole with constituent parts.

27. A *lexemic tagmeme* is one of the constituents of a lexemic construction, and includes features of lexemic arrangement and situation, with intersecting lexemic function and filler.
    27a. Tentatively, subject to major revision, we suggest (see Fig. 4) that *lexemic arrangement slot* may be used to refer to a place for a part in a larger whole; that the *lexemic filler class* has reference to

	Function	Filler
Arrangement	Slot (place of part in a whole)	Class (taxonomic)
Situation	Role (concept)	Category (paraphrase set)

Figure 4
Lexemic tagmeme

a taxonomic class filling one of these slots; that a *lexemic situational role* refers to a functional concept, and that the *lexemic filler category* may refer to a paraphrase set chosen to represent a subset of a taxonomic class of lexical units which carries the desired concept for the appropriate slot in some particular discourse.

28. The grammatical, phonological, and lexemic hierarchies intersect by sharing some characteristics of some lexical unit or units.

28a. The grammatical hierarchy has its morpheme or morpheme sequence — or a poem — as a basic unit; the same item is manifested by phonological units; and some one sense of that item is manifested by a paraphrase set of the lexemic hierarchy.

28b. The interface between manifested grammatical, phonological, and lexemic hierarchies, is the lexical hierarchy, of successively larger particular morpheme sequences.

28c. Two items from the same filler class of the grammatical hierarchy are not necessarily in the same lexemic class.
[Compare *her child* with *her singing*, with both as members of the noun-phrase class, but one in a conceptual taxonomic hierarchy of child-to-person, the other in vocal-to-general act.]

28d. Two items from the same lexemic class may be members of different grammatical filler classes.
[Compare *she sang* as an independent clause, with *her having sung* as a nominal. It is here that semantic sameness of situation can be seen in relation to grammatical differences of arrangement.]

28e. The grammatical and lexemic hierarchies also intersect in that lexemic concepts comprise the meaning attributed to the grammatical hierarchical pairs.
[Thus 'proposition' as a conceptual label comes from the lexemic hierarchy and is broader than the grammatical usage for independent clause or sentence, since it may also apply, for example, to propositions of dependent clauses.]

29. An abbreviated (incomplete) notation for the interaction between the grammatical, phonological, and lexemic hierarchies in some one tagmeme of some one particular speech act can be obtained (i) by starting with the grammatical four-cell notation of that tagmeme, (ii) adding to it a third column to give an INSTANCE of that tagmeme in the discourse in view, and (iii) adding a third row, to give the phonological arrangement of that instance; the cell of the intersection of arrangement row with instance column would include the lexical unit in view; the cell at the intersection of situation row and instance

120

column would contain the concept with sample members of its paraphrase set; the cell at the intersection of the phonological arrangement row and instance column would contain a phonemic representation of the lexical unit from the upper row, as it appears in the particular context from which it is taken.

[This nine-cell array has been useful to show the grammatical derivation of forms cited. It omits various elements which are simultaneously present.]

30. In certain special instances, where the BORDERS of the three hierarchies coincide, a fuller notation of a particular form as embedded in a particular discourse could presumably be shown with a three-tagmeme display (grammatical, phonological, lexemic) in which a single lexical unit simultaneously manifests the three tagmeme types. (See Fig. 5.)

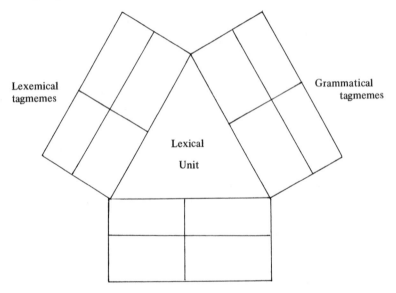

Figure 5

*Intersection of co-terminal lexemic, grammatical, and
phonological tagmemes in a lexical unit.*

[The usefulness of this display has not yet been tested.]

Bee, 1973, has a diagram with 'language' as its central triangle and with further triangles on its various sides representing the feature mode as semantics, distribution mode as syntax, and manifestation mode as phonology; these in turn continue with further triangles, in a variety of emic progressions. For difficulties with some kinds of emic progression, see Pike, 1967b: 515-17.

    30a. When the borders of the hierarchies do not coincide, separate displays must be given for parts of the sequence to be broken into different constituent parts depending upon the hierarchy under view.

31.   The interlocking hierarchies comprise a system of hierarchies.

32.   We speak of a *norm* for a unit (or its *normal variant*) when it is manifested by its most frequent variant; or by its nonfused variant; or when its borders are simultaneously borders of the grammatical, phological, and lexemic slots which it is filling, wholly or in part; (i.e. when they are *co-terminous*) or when that variant serves as a convenient starting place for rules to predict other variants.

    32a. Since the differing criteria sometimes lead to different analytical results, there is an *indeterminacy* as to the presence or boundaries of a norm; when the results coincide, certainty as to the presence and the identification of a norm increases.

    32b. In analytical work, norms are exploited in order to be able to find a convenient heuristic entrance into a complex system.
[That is, some complexities can be ignored by holding certain aspects of the system temporarily invariant, by use of norms.]

    32c. When two or more phonologically different variants of a lexical unit occur, the variants are *morphophonemically different variants*.
[We have now touched upon that part of our basic set of concepts which includes among them the following list in Fig. 6.]

Unit	Hierarchy	Context
Contrast	Lexemic	Form-meaning composite
Variation	Phonological	Change via shared component
Distribution	Grammatical	Universe of discourse
in Class		
in Sequence		
in System		

Figure 6
List of certain key tagmemic concepts minus particle, wave, field

33.   Observers both native and foreign may select any item or aspect of an item (or combination of items or aspects of items) of a system for explicit attention and analysis; this selection we will call *analytical focus*.

122

33a. Analytical focus may occur in various degrees on a continuum from explicit treatment (in *primary focus*) to subsidiary attention (*secondary* or *tertiary* focus), to tacit *presupposition* (unstated and *out of focus*).

[More than one degree of focus may be involved in a single statement, with lexemic, grammatical, or phonological clues to the items to be viewed in the various degrees. In *the decaying HOUSE* primary attention is on the unit 'house'; secondary attention is on the process of decay; in *the deCAYing house*, phonology switches focus to the process.]

33b. The analyst's choice, not the data, determines which hierarchy within a particular language at a particular time, and which levels of this chosen hierarchy (or hierarchies) will be explicit or tacit in that description; each presupposes a rudimentary other. For example one can concentrate at the level of discourse, calling it *discourse analysis* (or the *linguistic study of literature*); or at the level of the word, calling it *morphology*. Levels comprise a *system of levels* with interlocking features and definitions.

34. When primary analytical focus is on items in relation to contrast, variation, and distribution, focus is on emic units.

34a. When this type of focus and description is itself under primary attention (rather than the description of the units themselves) it may be called a *particle view*;

34b. When such a view is carried to an extreme, it may attempt to abstract the presentation of the units from their inevitable setting in time, hence appearing to be *static*.

[But note that tagmemics resists this exaggerated approach, requiring that every unit, to be well-defined, must have its distributional place in sequence specified; i.e. the time element is tacitly present even when a particle view is primary.]

35. When the analyst has primarily under attention certain sequence characteristics, versus marginal elements, and when he gives primary attention to the nuclei versus margins, or to the fact of the merging of these units in a larger unit rather than to their attempted abstraction from sequence or system, this view may be called *a dynamic perspective*.

35a. Presentation of units under the dynamic view does not require sharp segmentation at their borders; if the presence of two units can be known by their separate nuclei their borders may overlap or fuse without upsetting the analysis; and even their nuclei may under special circumstances merge such that *simultaneous units* (*portmanteau*) may occur.

35b. Since the succession of nucleus-margin-nucleus gives an appearance of flowing change, tagmemicists sometimes call this view a *wave perspective*.

35c. In the wave view, a segment is identified by a change, from less to more, or from more to less, of such aspects as DEGREE OF ARTICULATORY OPENNESS (e.g. in phonology), or independence (cf. grammar) or centrality of meaning (cf. lexical senses).
[Cf. K.L. Pike 1943a: 107 for underlying phonetic segment definition.]

35d. The wave view is tied closely to hierarchical concepts, as particle view was to concepts of the unit.

36. When analytical attention is primarily focused on the interdependent characteristics of a system, the view may be called a *relational perspective*, or a *field perspective*.

36a. The interdependence of elements focused on by a relational view are often conveniently presented in the form of a chart (or array) of intersecting rows and columns, each of which implies one feature of a relationally-viewed system, and the intersection of which results in a unit of that relationally-viewed system. Such a chart may be called a *component-times-component matrix*, or a *feature matrix*.

36b Every unit may be viewed as occurring at a point in a relationally-viewed system.

36c. Every unit may itself be viewed as a relational system, with its internal features seen as a set of intersecting elements.

36d. Every system, on the other hand, may be itself viewed as an emic unit such that the system, though defined in part by its internal set of relations, is for the moment primarily viewed as an entity in reference to its distribution in a larger unit.
[Cf. a system of traffic lights discussed as a whole.]

36e. Similarly, every system may be treated in a dynamic way, e.g. by noting how its nuclear characteristics are seen to change over time.

37. These perspectives can be reflected in the analyst's choice of descriptive frame of reference. Here the frame of reference is itself viewed as an emic unit of the analyst's behavior, which, in turn, can be viewed from the standpoint of the three perspectives.

37a. When pure relational elements are the analyst's ideal elements of the descriptive system, a NETWORK of relations is his ideal

124

description.
[Cf. the work or philosophy of some stratificationalists.]

37b. When dynamic elements are the analyst's ideal elements of his descriptive system (dynamic relative to the internal workings of the abstract descriptive mechanism, not relative to purported working of the data as such), a set of RULES may comprise his ideal output.
[Cf. the work of some transformationalists.]

37c. When static elements are the analyst's ideal elements of his descriptive system, an INVENTORY of units may comprise his ideal output.
[Cf. the work of some structuralists.]

37d. Tagmemics is a theory of the structure of human behavior (i) which attempts to preserve the three perspectives within a single frame of references, in a *complementarity* of perspectives which are static, dynamic, or relational (the tagmemicist affirms that on occasion each must be used if the analyst wishes to capture certain aspects of the behavior of the analyst or of the native performer); and (ii) which utilizes the concepts of unit, hierarchy, and context as indicated here.

37e. For the native speaker, the normal perspective – the most frequent under most situations – is probably the static one as primary, with dynamic and relational perspectives as potentially secondary or tertiary; but for special purposes, he may use any one in primary focus, with the others lowered in focus.

37f. An observer acting as analyst, using one or more of these perspectives in a systematic way, may be called a *scientist*; a science of language can be developed from any of these views, or any combination of them. Tagmemics, however, insists upon the essentiality of static, dynamic, and relational complementarity. This insistence, perhaps more than any other feature, currently differentiates tagmemics from other available theories of language or of language within behavior.
[And at this point we have reached our stated goal of introducing the concepts of particle, wave, and field, upon the basis of a prior introduction of unit, hierarchy, and context (rather than using the opposite order).]

REFERENCES

Ballard, D. Lee, Robert J. Conrad, and Robert E. Longacre
1971   "The deep and surface grammar of interclausal relations." *Foundations of Language* 7, 70-118.
Becker, Alton Lewis
1967   *A generative description of the English subject tagmeme* (PhD Dissertation: University of Michigan).
Bee, Darlene
1973   *Neo-Tagmemics*, ed. by Alan Healy and Doreen Marks, Summer Institute of Linguistics: Papua New Guinea
Beekman. John, and John Callow,
1975   *Translating the Word of God* (Grand Rapids: Zondervan)
Bernstein, Jared and Kenneth L. Pike
1974   "The emic structure of individuals in relation to dialogue", *Grammars and descriptions*, ed. by Teun A. van Dijk and Janos S. Petöfi (Amsterdam: University of Amsterdam)
Bloomfield, Leonard
1933   *Language* (New York: Holt).
Bold, Richard D.
1972   *A mathematical description of tagmemics* (PhD dissertation: University of Minnesota).
Brend, Ruth
1970   "Tagmemic theory: An annotated bibliography", *Journal of English Linguistics* 4, 7-46.
1972   "Tagmemic theory: An annotated bibliography, Appendix 1", *Journal of English Linguistics* 6, 1-16.
Chenowith, Vida and Darlene Bee
1971   "Comparative-generative models of a New Guinea Melodic structure", *American Anthrpologist* 73, 773-782.
Cook, Walter A., S.J.
1970   "Case grammar: From roles to rules", *Languages and Linguistics: Working Papers 1*, 14-29. (Washington D.C.: Georgetown University).
1971a   "Case grammar as a deep structure in tagmemic analysis", *Languages and Linguistics: Working Papers*, 2, 1-9. (Washington D.C.: Georgetown University).
1971b   "Improvements in case grammar 1970", *Languages and Linguistics: Working Papers 2*, 10-22. (Washington D.C. Georgetown University).
Crawford, John C.
1963   *Totontepec Mixe phonotagmemics* (Sa nta Ana: Summer Institute of Linguistics Publications in Linguistics and Related Fields No. 8).
Elson, Benjamin and Velma B. Pickett
1962   *An introduction to morphology and syntax* (Santa Ana: Summer Institute of Linguistics).
Fillmore, Charles
1968   "The case for case", in *Universals in linguistics theory,* Ed. by E Bach and R. Harms. (New York: Holt, Rinehart and Winston), 1-88.
Forster, Jannette
1964   "Dual structure in Dibabawon verbal clauses", *Oceanic Linguistics,* 3:26-48.
Fries, Charles
1952   *The structure of English* (New York: Harcourt, Brace and Co.).
Fries, Peter
1970   *Tagmeme sequences in the English noun phrase* (Santa Ana: Summer

126

Institute of Linguistics Publications in Linguistics and Related Fields No. 36).

Hale, Austin
  1973   *Clause, Sentence, and Discourse Patterns in Selected languages of Nepal*, Huntington Beach: Summer Institute of Linguistics Publications in Linguistics and Related Fields, 40)
Huttar, George
  1973   'On destinguishing clause and sentence', *Linguistics* 105. 69-82.
Klammer, Thomas Paul
  1971   *The structure of dialogue paragraphs in written English dramatic and narrative discourse* (Phd Dissertstion, University of Michigan).
Larsón, Mildred
  1975   *Practice manual of drills* (Grand Rapids: Zondervan).
Longacre, Robert
  1964   *Grammar discovery procedures: a field manual* (=Janua Linguarum, Series Minor 33) (The Hague: Mouton).
  1968   *Discourse, paragraph and sentence structure in selected Philippine languages* Vol. 1, Vol. 2. (U.S. Office of Education, Institute of International Studies). [Also Summer Institute of Linguistics [Santa Ana] Publications in Linguistics, 21]
  1972   *Hierarchy and Universality of Discourse Constituents in New Guinea Languages* Vol. I, *Discussion*; Vol II, *Texts* (Washington: Georgetown University Press).
Merrifield, William, Constance Naish and Calvin Rensch
  1960   *Lab manual for beginning morphology and syntax* (Santa Ana: Summer Institute of Linguistics).
Pickett, Velma Bernice
  1960   *The grammatical hierarchy of Isthmus Zapotec, Language Dissertation* 56. [PhD Dissertation, University of Michigan)]
Pike, Kenneth L.
  1943a   *Phonetics: A critical analysis of phonetic theory and a technique for the practical description of sounds*, University of Michigan Publications in Language and Literature, 21. (Ann Arbor, University of Michigan).
  1943b   "Taxemes and immediate constituents", *Language*, 19. 65-82.
  1944   "Analysis of a Mixteco text", *International Journal of American Linguistics 10*, 113-138.
  1947   *Phonemics: A technique for reducing languages to writing* (University of Michigan Publications in Linguistics 3) Ann Arbor: University of Michigan Press). [First Mimeo'd edition 1943]
  1958   "On tagmemes née gramemes", *International Journal of American Linguistics*, 24.273-78.
  1959   "Language as particle, wave and field", *Texas Quarterly* 2.2.37-54.
  1962   "Dimensions of grammatical constructions", *Language* 38.221-244.
  1963   "Theoretical implications of matrix permutations in Fore", *Anthropological Linguistics* 5,8.1-23.
  1964a   "A linguistic contribution to composition", *Journal of the Conference on College Composition and Communication* 15.82-88.
  1964b   "Discourse analysis and tagmeme matrices", *Oceanic Linguistics* 3.1.5.-25.
  1964c   "Beyond the sentence", *Journal of Conference on College Composition and Communication*, 15.129-135.
  1965   "Language, where science and poetry meet", *College English* 26.283-292.
  1966   "A guide to publications related to tagmemic theory" in *Current Trends in Linguistics* Vol. III, ed. by Thomas Sebeok (The Hague: Mouton), 365-94.
  1967a   "Grammar as wave", *Monograph Series on Languages and Linguistics* 20

(Georgetown University: Institute of Languages and Linguistics) 1-14.

1967b   *Language in relation to a unified theory of the structure of human behavior*, Second, Revised Edition, (Mouton and Company: The Hague) [1954, 1955, 1960, Parts I, II and III. Preliminary Edition (Glendale [now Huntington Beach], California, Summer Institute of Linguistics).]

1971a   "Crucial questions in the development of tagmemics – the sixties and seventies" *Monograph Series on Languages and Linguistics 24* (Georgetown University Institute of Languages and Linguistics), 79-98.

1971b   "Implications of the patterning of an oral reading of a set of poems", *Poetics*, 1.38-45.

1973a   "Science fiction as a test of axioms concerning human behavior" *Parma Eldalamberon* No. 3. 3-4. 6-7.

1973b   "Sociolinguistic evaluation of alternative mathematical models: English pronouns", *Language* 49, 121, 160.

Pike Kenneth L. and Barbara Erickson

1964   "Conflated field structures in Potawatomi and Arabic" *International Journal of American Linguistics*, 30.201-212.

Pike Kenneth L. and Ivan Lowe

1969   "Pronominal reference in English conversation and discourse: a group theoretical treatment", *Folia Linguistica* 3, 68-106.

Pike, Kenneth L. and Evelyn G. Pike

1972   "Seven substitution exercises for studying the structure of discourse" *Linguistics* 94.43-52.

[1975]   *Grammatical analysis* (mimeo'd Edition).

Platt, Heidi

1970   *A comparative study of English and German syntax*, PhD dissertation, Monash University.

Platt, John

1971   *Grammatical form and grammatical meaning*, [PhD Dissertation, 1970, Monash University] (Amsterdam: North-Holland Publishing Co.)

Poythress, Vern

1973   "A formalism for describing rules of conversation", *Semiotica* 7.285-299.

Tench, Paul

1972   (manuscript) *A paired-level hierarchy in phonology*, [A paper presented to the Research Seminar in Phonetics and Linguistics, Cardiff, 1972.]

Trager, George

1949   *The field of linguistics. (Studies in Linguistics Occasional papers*, No. 1)

Trail, Ronald

1973   *Patterns in clause, sentence, and discourse in selected languages of India and Nepal* (Santa Ana: Summer Institute of Linguistics Publications in Linguistics and Related Fields 41.).

Wise, Mary Ruth

1971   *Identification of participants in discourse: A study of form and meaning in Nomatsiguenga*. Santa Ana: Summer Institute of Linguistics Publications in Linguistics and Related Fields 28. [PhD Dissertation, University of Michigan 1968].

Wise, Mary Ruth and Ivan Lowe

1972   Permutation groups in discourse, *Working papers in languages and linguistics* No. 4, 12-34. (Washington D.C. Georgetown University). [PhD dissertation, Univ. of Michigan, 1968.]

INDEX

130

ture 19, 44, 52, 83
definition 105, 116
deletion 2
dependent 10, 110
derivation 60, 62, 63, 66, 69
description 75
development 8, 9
dialog 10, 110
dictionary 117
Dik, S. 86
discourse 11, 12, 47, 100, 102, 119
discovery procedure 94
distinctive feature 99
distribution 68, 92, 96, 101, 109, 110
dominance 83
double-function 2, 35, 38-39
Dravidian 99
dynamic 91, 99-100, 122, 123

elicitation 110
Elson, B. 2, 8, 39, 47, 102, 125
emic 69, 91-93, 112-116, 123
emic feature 60, 66, 67, 75, 80
empiricism 75
encounter 110
English 6, 9, 11, 12, 16, 17, 19, 20, 32,
40, 41, 46, 53-66, 72, 79, 82
Erickson. B. 99, 127
etic 15, 71, 91, 102, 113
exchange 110
expansion 66, 110, 115
experience 69
exponence 76

feature 23, 24, 40-43, 111-113, 123
field 42-43, 69, 93, 123
filler 61, 97, 98, 109, 114, 118, 119
filler, lexemic 118
Fillmore, C. J. 12-13, 43, 47, 72, 73,
87, 99, 125
focus 30, 47, 116, 121, 122
Fodor, J. A. 87
form 2, 4, 6, 8, 24, 25, 42, 46, 60, 64,
67, 68, 69, 94, 111
form-meaning composite 2, 3, 25, 111-
113
formalism 37-41, 51-52, 75, 76, 104
formula 38, 61, 62, 76
Forster, J. 99, 125
frame 109
frame of reference 111
Franklin, K. J. 86, 87
free 112
Fries, C. C. 116, 125

Fries, P. H. 1, 20, 48, 82, 87, 100, 104
function 1-6, 24, 25, 35, 38, 41, 42, 44,
45, 60, 65, 72, 81, 96, 98, 114, 125
fusion 98

generalization 38
generation 76, 82
generic 118
grameme 95
grammar 2-5, 14, 32-37, 44, 52, 72, 102-
103, 114
Greenbaum, S. 49
Grimes, J. E. 75, 87

Hale, A. 12, 13, 26, 33, 34, 45, 46, 48,
51, 74, 82, 99, 125
Halliday, M. A. K. 19, 34, 48
Harris, Z. S. 82, 83, 87
Hart, H. L. 47, 48
heuristic 6, 41, 99, 102, 104, 113, 122
hierarchy 34, 42, 59, 60, 68, 70, 71, 76,
92-93, 96-98, 101-104, 110-111, 114-
116, 118-122
hierarchy, grammatical 6, 119
hierarchy, interlocking 119-121
hierarchy, lexemic 119
hierarchy, phonological 114, 116, 119
Hollenbach, B. E. 39, 48
homophony 117
Householder, F. 86
Huttar, G. 101, 103, 125

idea 45
identification 113
immediate constituent 69, 94
independent 110
indeterminacy 91, 99, 121
Indo-European 99
initiator 110
insertion 63, 64
intensifier 44
interaction 111, 115
intuition 93
issue 112
item 108, 110-112, 121

Jacobs, K. 40, 48, 68, 78, 79, 87

Katz, J. J. 87
Klammer, T. P. 67, 73, 81, 82, 88, 100,
125

Lakoff, G. 14, 48

131

Lamani 43
Larson, M. 99, 102, 125
Leech, G. 49
Lees, R. B. 83, 88
level 6, 12, 41, 42, 69-71, 80, 104, 115,
116, 118, 122
level-skipping 44
lexeme, see lexemic structure
lexemic, see lexemic structure
lexemic structure 4, 13, 23-25, 32-34, 36,
37, 43, 101, 102, 115, 117, 118, 119
lexical, see lexemic structure 81
lexicon 72
Liem, N. D. 6, 48
Longacre, R. E. 2, 4, 5, 8, 12, 15, 18-20,
24, 40, 42, 43, 47-49, 59, 68-71, 76-
-79, 83, 86-88, 95, 100, 103, 126
Lowe, I. 102, 104, 127

Manandhar, T. 75, 87
manifestation 2, 72, 114
margin 62, 66
matrix 26, 42-43, 78, 92, 99, 123
meaning 2-5, 8, 10-11, 19, 21, 25, 31,
42, 44, 46, 64, 67-69, 72, 92-94, 98,
99, 102, 103, 111, 115, 117
member 109
Merrifield. W. R. 80, 81, 86, 88, 102,
126
message 3
minimum 110, 115
modality 19, 21, 44
modals 53-66
modification 20-22, 34, 35, 43-45
morpheme 60, 96-97, 114, 117
morpheme cluster 115
morphophonemic 56, 58
multiple function 36
Munda 99

Naish, C. 126
native speaker 91
negative 56, 57
neighbor 111, 112
neighborhood 110-111
New Guinea 99
nominalization 36, 37, 43
non-contrastive 112
non-verbal behavior 1, 91-92, 109
non-verbal element 75-76
norm 121
North American Indian 99
noun 43, 44
noun phrase 20-22, 36-37, 41, 44, 45,

79, 100
number 54, 57

object 32, 83
objects 46
obligatory 116
observer 69, 41, 93, 108-112, 121
occurrence 109
operations 76-77
optional 116
ordering 109

paradigm 29, 30, 46, 113
paraphrase 117, 118
participant 15, 20, 26, 32, 43, 67, 109
particle 69, 93, 122
puase group 114
perception 108
performer 42
permutation 76, 77, 79, 83
person 108
perspective 67, 69, 76, 93, 124
phoneme 96, 114, 116
phoneme cluster 116
phonetics 97
phonological tagmeme 116
phonology 97, 101, 103-104
phrase 8, 9, 20-22, 24, 34, 35, 41, 43,
44, 61, 65, 115
phrase-structure grammar 38-39
phrase structure rules 53
Pickett, V. B. 2, 8, 39, 47, 100, 102, 125,
126
Pike, E. G. 8, 9, 12, 14, 15, 26, 30, 31,
35, 36, 41, 43, 45, 46, 48, 59, 60, 64-
-67, 73-75, 79, 82, 83, 89, 101-104, 127
Pike, K. L. 3, 8-12, 14, 15, 24-26, 30, 35,
36, 40-43, 45-48, 51, 59, 60, 64-67, 72-
-75, 79, 82, 83, 88-91, 99, 100-103,
120, 125-127
Platt, H. 99, 127
Platt, J. T. 12, 48, 49, 72, 127
poem 100
portmanteau 122
position 94, 95, 98
possessive 37
Postal, P. M. 38, 48, 82, 83, 89
postulates, tagmemic 104-124
Poythress, V. 102, 127
predicate 6, 8, 45
predication 12, 15, 45
prepositional phrase 41
preposition 9, 10, 14, 16-17, 19, 21, 22,
33, 43, 44, 103, 115, 118, 119